Three Plays of
Tirso de Molina

Three Plays of Tirso de Molina

New Translations of
Don Juan: The Jackal of Seville;
A Sinner Saved, a Saint Damned; and
The Timid Young Man at the Palace Gate

Translated by
Raymond Conlon

McFarland & Company, Inc., Publishers
Jefferson, North Carolina

LIBRARY OF CONGRESS CATALOGUING-IN-PUBLICATION DATA

Names: Molina, Tirso de, 1571?-1648 author. | Conlon, Raymond translator.
Title: Three plays of Tirso de Molina : new translations of Don Juan, the jackal of Seville; A sinner saved, a saint damned; and The timid young man at the palace gate / translated by Raymond Conlon.
Description: Jefferson, North Carolina : McFarland & Company, Inc., Publishers, 2017. | Includes bibliographical references and index.
Identifiers: LCCN 2017016904 | ISBN 9781476666549 (softcover : acid free paper) ∞
Classification: LCC PQ6435.E5 T57 2017 | DDC 862/.3—dc23
LC record available at https://lccn.loc.gov/2017016904

BRITISH LIBRARY CATALOGUING DATA ARE AVAILABLE

ISBN (print) 978-1-4766-6654-9
ISBN (ebook) 978-1-4766-2853-0

© 2017 Raymond Conlon. All rights reserved

No part of this book may be reproduced or transmitted in any form or by any means, electronic or mechanical, including photocopying or recording, or by any information storage and retrieval system, without permission in writing from the publisher.

Front cover image © 2017 Garsya/iStock

Printed in the United States of America

McFarland & Company, Inc., Publishers
  Box 611, Jefferson, North Carolina 28640
    www.mcfarlandpub.com

For Anne and Gabriel

Table of Contents

General Introduction: Tirso de Molina
   (Gabriel Téllez), 1580?–1648   1
Notes on the Translation   7
Texts of Plays Consulted   9

Don Juan: The Jackal of Seville   11
A Sinner Saved, a Saint Damned   66
The Timid Young Man at the Palace Gate   109

General Introduction: Tirso de Molina (Gabriel Téllez), 1580?–1648

Tirso's Life and Clerical Career

Extensive research over centuries has yielded an inconclusive picture of the life of Tirso de Molina. We know that he was born Gabriel de Téllez in Madrid. The date is a matter of dispute, though it is popularly believed to have been around 1579 or 1580.

Likewise, there is debate about who his parents were. The preeminent student of his life, the Reverend Luis Vásquez, identifies Tirso's father and mother as Andrés López and Juana Téllez, and claims he had a sister, Catalina Téllez. Another scholar asserts that Tirso was the illegitimate child of the second Duke of Osuna, Juan Téllez Girón, Count of Ureña.

We know almost nothing about Tirso's childhood. Some biographers believe Tirso attended the University of Alcalá de Henares, but there is no concrete evidence supporting that notion.

A central fact of Tirso's biography is that he was a priest, and from reliable Church records we can trace his clerical career. He joined the Mercedarian order in 1600, and was ordained in 1608. For eight years after that he pursued his religious studies and duties in various locales within Spain.

In 1616 Tirso set out for the Dominican Republic, where he would assume an administrative post of his order. He returned to Madrid in 1618, remaining for seven years. After that Tirso spent time serving in different provincial posts. He would eventually become the historian of the Mercedarian order, composing the *Historia general de la orden de la Merced* in 1637. Tirso de Molina died in February 1648.

General Introduction

Tirso's Dramatic Career

Of course our main interest in Tirso is his career as a dramatist, and, as with his life, some important facts elude us. Two outstanding problems prevent a secure understanding of his work: We are unsure about the authorship of several plays attributed to him, including two here, and uncertain about the chronology of many of his works.

Despite these significant gaps, we have a general picture of the parabola of Tirso's dramatic career. We do know that he began composing plays in the first decade of the seventeenth century. His first work was probably *The Timid Young Man at the Palace Gate*, written around 1606. Between 1606 and 1625 his literary career burgeoned. It was a period of remarkable activity, during which he composed hundreds of plays and achieved a reputation as an important dramatist.

The high regard Tirso garnered in those extraordinarily fruitful nineteen years is at least partially attributable to the fact that he revealed a gift largely absent in other contemporary Spanish dramatists: the ability to create subtle and psychologically complex characters. His female figures in particular demonstrate a singular vitality and emotional complexity. Indeed, his perceptive treatment of women and his frank treatment of their sexuality probably contributed to his being censured in 1625 for the worldly character of his plays. Soon after this censure, his dramatic production largely came to an end.

The Spanish Theater in the Time of Tirso

Tirso wrote during the Spanish Golden Age, the era in which art and literature flourished as at no other time in the history of Spain. Lasting from 1500 to 1680, it produced Cervantes, Velázquez, Murillo, John of the Cross, Teresa of Ávila, and the Escorial. This was a stunningly productive period in the history of Spanish theater: The number of plays penned by the three greatest dramatists of the era, Lope de Vega (Félix Lope de Vega y Carpio; 1562–1635), Pedro Calderón de la Barca (1600–1681), and Tirso, is well over a thousand.

The seed of this dramatic fertility was necessity. The theater was an immensely popular form of entertainment for all classes and both sexes.

General Introduction

Dramatists had to construct pleasing distractions on a nearly weekly basis, as each play was only performed a handful of times.

A speech reflecting the popular enthusiasm for the theater appears in *The Timid Young Man at the Palace Gate.*

> What satisfaction is to be found in a celebration or a game that you can't discover in the theater? Doesn't the theater offer you pleasure and present a thousand gifts that make you forget your troubles? Is not the ear entertained by its music? The clever fellow enjoys its wit and subtlety, the jolly man finds laughter, the gloomy one discovers sorrow, the sharp one encounters biting wit. Doesn't the stubborn fellow get a warning and the ignorant one a lesson? And the bravo, doesn't he find wars, and the prudent, counsel? If you want to see Moors, there are Moors; if you crave tournaments, there you can find them; if bulls, a bullfight.
>
> These are some of the epithets I've found best for the drama: copy of life, food of the wits, beloved lady of the intellect, banquet of the senses, bouquet of different tastes, sphere of the mind, Lethe washing away sorrows, and, finally, a delicacy, that, bought at different prices, starves the foolish and satisfies the wise.

The formula for this popular entertainment is often credited to one playwright: Lope de Vega. He created character types that could be used, with slight variations, over and over. These included the dashing *galán* and his comic sidekick (the *gracioso*), the lovely *dama*, the timid cleric, the rakish seducer, and the humble peasant (the *villano*) with a noble heart.

Lope and other playwrights also fashioned dramatic plots that could be endlessly recycled. Two of the most popular were the "cape and sword" and the "honor" plays. In light-hearted "cape and sword" dramas a *galán* pursues an eligible *dama*. Courtship often includes disguises, swordplay, and confusion. These plays usually end well, boy gets girl. Honor plays involve an illicit affair on the part of a man's wife. The "honor code" demanded that the husband slay not only his rival but also his wife. The climactic conclusion of these dramas is almost always a bloody one. The drawing power of these plays is such that some mention the theme in their titles, such as Calderón's *The Surgeon of his Honor* and *The Painter of his Honor.*

Other typical plays of the era deal with religion, such as hagiographies and allegories, as well as Spanish history. Interludes (*entremeses*), one-act comedies played between acts of longer works, were also popular, as were humorous romantic plays involving confusion and disguise.

Tirso de Molina was very much a dramatist of his time. In particular, he was a literary disciple of Lope de Vega, employing similar character types, themes, and plots. Tirso also enlisted in Lope's innovative rebellion against Renaissance drama's classicism: He combines tragic and comic elements, violates the Aristotelian unities of time and place, and mixes low and high characters. Tirso also follows Lope's dramatic structure, rejecting the Renaissance five-act play in favor of a straightforward, simple, and lively three-act one: Present the problem in Act One, develop the problem in Act Two, solve the problem in Act Three.

Nondramatic Poets and Tirso

During the Golden Age the Spanish literary world was under the spell of the Baroque poet Luis de Góngora (1561–1627). Góngora's verse is often labeled *culto* or cultured, his movement *culteranismo*. His poetry is elaborate, complicated, with Latinate-like syntax and complex, often confusing metaphorical constructions. Though not usually associated with Góngora, Tirso's writing sometimes evinces the influence of his style. We can see an example of it in a passage from *A Sinner Saved, A Saint Damned*. A literal translation would read something like this: "The woman began to scream and I, taking out my sword, placed it five or six times in the crystal of her breast where portals of rubies on beautiful crystal fields gave an exit for her soul to flee her body." Another major non-dramatic writer whose influence appears in Tirso's work is Francisco de Quevedo (1580–1645), who is associated with a device called *"conceptismo."* His verse, highly intellectual and often satirical, frequently contains different meanings of the same word or phrase, and the extended development of a conceit, a *concepto*.

The King and God in Golden Age Theater

At the core of the works of Tirso, Lope, or most other Golden Age dramatists is a profound conservatism. The two pillars of Golden Age theater are the Monarchy and the Church. Plays over and over extol and defend these institutions, reminding audiences that the stability of the society and the well-being of its people depend on them.

General Introduction

Medieval and Renaissance Spanish kings and queens appear in various sorts of plays, not just histories, and are characteristically depicted in a favorable, often laudatory light. Customarily, kings are sagacious in statecraft, brave in war, pious in their faith, and devoted in their domestic lives; queens are loving and judicious advisors to their spouses. The singular importance of the monarch does not depend on virtue, however. Even when a king is not a moral paragon—a royal seducer in an honor play, for example—his indispensable social and political role makes him inviolable, exempting him from the otherwise inevitable fatal punishment of the honor code.

Golden Age plays often display the price of sin, and as to God's punishment, there are no exemptions. Sin is punished and punishment is just. Two figures from different plays in this collection are dragged down to hell. The Golden Age audience would waste no time pitying them; rather, it would see their punishment as the logical and morally coherent end to misspent lives. The moral ambiguities we see in Greek and Shakespearean tragedies, in which heroes endure punishments disproportionate to their misdeeds, have little place in Spanish Golden Age religious drama. Not surprisingly, the three greatest playwrights of the Golden Age theater—Lope, Tirso, and Calderón—were priests.

Tirso's Influence

Despite the fact that there are extant about eighty-five plays attributed to Tirso, his influence on literature outside the Spanish reading world can be summed up in two words: Don Juan. Paradoxically, within that delimitation his influence has been enormous. Poets, dramatists, and composers from various eras and national traditions have been struck by the artistic and psychological possibilities of Don Juan and molded the figure to make him their own—Mozart, Molière, Byron, Shaw, and Pushkin, to name a few. Indeed, the appeal of Don Juan is such that the name is a common noun.

That Tirso's influence is limited to the Don Juan figure is easily explainable. Until recently few translations of his works existed. As the number increases, his importance will expand and his talent will be more widely recognized.

GENERAL INTRODUCTION

The Plays Translated Here

The three plays in this collection are generally considered among his most important. *Don Juan: The Jackal of Seville* and *A Sinner Saved, a Saint Damned* are popularly regarded as his masterpieces, *The Timid Youth at the Place Gate*, as one of the comic gems of the era. All reveal Tirso's singular gift among his contemporaries as a dramatic psychologist, creating convincing and powerful characters in *Don Juan* and *A Sinner Saved* and intriguing female figures in *The Timid Youth*. The psychological complexity and vitality of these characters, being unique to Tirso among Golden Age writers, produce works of enduring importance and refute whatever quibbles there might be about the authorship of any of the plays translated here.

Note on the Translation

My translation is neither an academically literal one nor a radically simplified theatrical version, but rather something between the two. It is in prose, which sometimes has the effect of shortening and simplifying the long and very complicated poetical texture of the Spanish, but still capturing, I believe, the beauty and spirit of the verse original.

Texts of Plays Consulted

El burlador de Sevilla
(*Don Juan: The Jackal of Seville*):

Editor: Américo Castro. Madrid: Clásicos castellanos. 1958.
Editor: Juan Manuel Oliver. Barcelona: Plaza y Janés. 1984.
Editor: James Parr. Binghamton, N.Y.: Medieval & Renaissance Texts and Studies. 1994.
Editor: Raymond MacCurdy. *Spanish Drama of the Golden Age*. Englewood Cliffs, New Jersey: Prentice-Hall. 1971.

El condenado por desconfiado
(*A Sinner Saved, a Saint Damned*):

Editor: Raymond MacCurdy. *Spanish Drama of the Golden Age*. Englewood Cliffs, New Jersey: Prentice-Hall. 1971.
Editor: Bruce Wardropper. *Teatro español del siglo de oro*. New York: Scribner's. 1970.

El vergonzoso en palacio
(*The Timid Young Man at the Palace Gate*):

Editor: Américo Castro. *Comedias* I, 9th edition. Madrid: Espasa-Calpe. 1970.
Editor: Everett Hesse. Madrid: Cátedra. 1976.
Editor: Blanca Oteiza. Madrid: Biblioteca clásica de la Real Academia Española, volume 62. 2012.

Don Juan: The Jackal of Seville
(published 1630)

As with so much concerning Tirso, there is considerable confusion concerning important aspects of his most famous play, *Don Juan: The Jackal of Seville*. For one thing, we are not sure that he wrote it, though scholarship traditionally holds him to be its author. We also do not know when the play was written. Finally, the popular notion that the Don Juan of this play is the ur–Don Juan is inaccurate—a somewhat similar figure existed in early ballads and in another contemporary play. One fact concerning the work, however, brooks no debate: The Don Juan of this play, whenever he was created, and whoever created him, is the best-known and most influential character of Spanish drama.

Although Tirso's Don Juan is the literary ancestor of the many other artistic figures that have the same name, he is fundamentally different from them. Typically, his descendants are sexually irresistible, often racking up conquest after conquest, as we hear in the boastful refrain of Mozart's Don Giovanni, "*in Spagna mille e tre*." The Jackal of Seville is not a great seducer. The number of women he sleeps with is a modest one: only three or perhaps four (one is unclear). Indeed, it is arguable he is not a seducer at all: He sleeps with two (or perhaps one) by impersonating their lovers, two by the promise of marriage.

The deviousness of Don Juan's amatory achievements suggests that his motive is not passion but the sheer love of deception, of humiliating women. Indeed, he says as much: "Tricks are my great joy ... my greatest pleasure is to shame a woman, depriving her of her honor." Don Juan is not a lover so much as a sadist.

Significantly, his cruelty is not limited to women. Two of the four women he seduces are the lovers of other men, a third is a bride. Perhaps Don Juan's cruelest deception is played on his friend, the Marqués de la

Mota. When the Marqués's beloved Ana gives Don Juan a note to deliver to his friend Mota, arranging an assignation at eleven, he tells Mota to arrive at twelve, just after Don Juan (impersonating Mota) is to leave Ana's bed. This is what Don Juan says to himself about his contemplated jest: "Unfortunate lover! Have you ever seen anything like it? This prank really makes me laugh."

There are many interpretations of Don Juan's motives for his cruelty. The number and variety of differing views about the "why" of Don Juan's cruelty is telling. It suggests that attributing the impulse for Don Juan's humiliations of unsuspecting men and women to a particular motive or psychological condition would be misguided, reductionistic. Rather, he appears to be driven to degrade others by the same mysterious "motiveless malignity" that Coleridge saw in Iago. The whole point of his cruelty is that there is no point to it.

The question of the protagonist's motivation is one that probably did not trouble—even concern—most Golden Age viewers of *Don Juan: The Jackal of Seville*. Contemporary playgoers viewed it primarily as a theological and didactic drama. Its theme was unmistakable: God punishes the unrepentant sinner. The playwright employs the protagonist's sidekick Catalinón to remind the audience over and over of the inevitability of infernal punishment for those who will not reform and repent. Catalinón tells his master and he tells us: "Look at what you've done, and look how short is even the longest life, and after death there is hell." Don Juan's father makes an even sterner admonition: "Traitor, may God punish you with suffering equal to your sin ... and though God seems to nod at your sins, your punishment will not be long in coming. And there is punishment for those who swear falsely in his name, for when death comes He is a harsh judge." These warnings to Don Juan of the danger of eternal punishment recall those of the chorus in Greek tragedies: They are ignored by the protagonist but not by the audience. They create a growing and increasingly intense sense of the inevitability of Don Juan's damnation.

Don Juan: The Jackal of Seville
Characters

Don Juan Tenorio
Catalinón: Sidekick of Don Juan
Don Diego Tenorio: Father of Don Juan
Don Pedro Tenorio: Ambassador of Spain in the court of the King of Naples and uncle of Don Juan
The King of Castile: Alfonso XI

The King of Naples
Isabela: Duchess
Fabio: Servant of Isabela
Duke Octavio
Ripio: Servant of Duke Octavio
Tisbea: Fisherwoman
Coridón: Fisherman
Anfriso: Fisherman
Fishermen
Don Gonzalo de Ulloa: Comendador of Calatrava
Doña Ana de Ulloa: Daughter of Don Gonzalo
The Marqués de la Mota
Aminta: Peasant woman
Batricio: Bridegroom of Aminta
Gaseno: Father of Aminta
Belisa: Friend of Aminta
Shepherds
Servants
Musicians
The Night Watch

The time: 14th century

Act I

[A very dark room in the palace of the King of Naples.]

(Enter Don Juan and Isabela.)

ISABELA: Duke Octavio, through here, it's safer.

DON JUAN: Duchess, again I swear I will carry out my sacred promise to you.

ISABELA: Now will my joys and glories finally come true and your promises be fulfilled.

DON JUAN: Yes, my love.

ISABELA: I'll get a candle.

DON JUAN: Why?

ISABELA: So my soul may see the joy I feel.

DON JUAN: Don't, I'll snuff out the light.

ISABELA: Oh, heaven, who are you, what man are you?

DON JUAN: Who am I? A man without a name.

ISABELA: You are not the Duke?

DON JUAN: No.

ISABELA: Help, let everyone in the palace be awakened!

DON JUAN: Stop this, Duchess. Give me your hand.

ISABELA: Don't try to stop me, villain. Let the King be called, soldiers, people!

(Enter the King of Naples with a candle in a holder.)

KING: What is this?

ISABELA (aside): *The King. Now I'm for it!*

KING: Who are you?

DON JUAN: Who should we be? A man and a woman.

KING (aside, seeing the Duchess): *This must be handled with tact.* Guard, seize this man!

ISABELA (aside): *My honor is lost!* (Exit.)

(Enter Don Pedro Tenorio, the Spanish Ambassador and guards.)

DON PEDRO: Voices in your rooms, Sire, what is the cause?

KING: Don Pedro Tenorio, I put this man in your hands. Discover his identity. I have just touched the surface of this affair, look into it in greater detail—and in secret, for there is the scent of scandal here. I have seen all I wish to see. (Exit.)

DON PEDRO: Seize him.

DON JUAN: Who dares try? I may lose my life, but it will cost someone dearly.

DON PEDRO: Kill him!

DON JUAN: Don't deceive yourself, I'm resolved to die. I am a nobleman and of the Spanish Embassy. Let the Ambassador approach, for it is only to him I shall yield.

DON PEDRO: Everyone to that room over there, and take the woman. (Exeunt the guards.)

DON PEDRO: Now the two of us are alone; show me your courage and your spirit.

DON JUAN: I possess courage but none for you.

DON PEDRO: Tell me, who are you?

DON JUAN: Your nephew.

DON PEDRO (aside): *Oh my God! I fear some treachery.* What have you done? Scoundrel! How could you act in this fashion? Tell me immediately what has happened. You disobedient ... reckless! ... I could kill you. Go on.

DON JUAN: Uncle, I am no different than you were at my age—you knew of passion then, so excuse mine now. And since you force me to speak, listen and I will tell you: Through a deception I took my pleasure of Isabela, the Duchess...

DON PEDRO: Don't go on. Stop. How did you deceive her? Speak in a quiet tone.

DON JUAN: I pretended to be Duke Octavio...

DON PEDRO: No more, that's enough ... (aside) *Should the King discover this, I'm lost. What shall I do? My wits must be my salvation in such a delicate situation.* Tell me, scoundrel, wasn't it bad enough you already committed such an outrage in Spain with a woman of your own rank; but here in Naples, in the royal palace with a woman of such a high position.... May God punish you! From Castile your father sent you across the sea to lovely Naples expecting that you would repay his graciousness. Instead you bring shame to him—and with a woman of such high rank! But time is working against us; what are you going to do?

DON JUAN: I make no excuse; to do so would be dishonorable. My blood is yours, shed it!—and I'll pay for my sin. I throw myself at your feet, and here you have my sword, sir.

DON PEDRO: Rise up, show courage; your humility has conquered me. Will you dare to drop from this balcony?

DON JUAN: Yes, your confidence emboldens me.

DON PEDRO: I'm on your side. Go to Sicily or Milan where you can live unrecognized.

DON JUAN: Then, I'm off.

DON PEDRO: My letters will let you know the outcome of this mess you caused.

DON JUAN (aside): *It wasn't so bad for me!* I admit my guilt in this matter.

DON PEDRO: It's your youth that makes you sin. Down, then, by this balcony.

DON JUAN: With such an agreeable purpose, joyfully, I'm off to Spain.

(Exit Don Juan.)

(Enter the King of Naples.)

DON PEDRO: I carried out your just and proper order, Sire, the man...

KING: Is dead?

DON PEDRO: Escaped, despite the proud sword opposing him.

KING: How could this happen?

DON PEDRO: Not a moment after you commanded me, saying nothing, clenching his sword, cape wrapped around his arm, in a flash he attacked the guards. Courting death the desperate figure, seeking to save himself, jumped from the balcony into the garden, your diligent men close behind. They pursued him to then nearby door where they found him wounded, at point of death, curled up like a snake, his face bathed in blood. Then, raising himself, the soldiers crying "kill him, kill him," he fled with such flashing speed I was left in stunned confusion. The woman Isabela—and I know that name must take you aback—is withdrawn to a nearby room. She identifies Don Octavio as her deceiver, her seducer.

KING: What do you say?

DON PEDRO: What she herself confessed.

KING (aside): *How sad is it that man's honor is his essence, but it hangs on the thread-like lightness of woman's fickleness?*

(Enter a servant.)

SERVANT: Great Sire!

KING: Bring the woman before me.

SERVANT: Now the guard comes with her, Sire.

[The Royal Guard brings Isabela before the King.]

ISABELA (aside): *How can I face the King?*

KING: Go and guard the doors to this room. (Exeunt the guards.)

Tell me, woman, what rage, what madness, or what falling star prompted you in your beauty and arrogance to profane the portals of my palace?

ISABELA: Sire...

KING: Silence, your tongue cannot smooth over your offense to me. The man fled was the Duke Octavio?

ISABELA: Sire...

KING: Nothing—fortresses, guards, servants, parapets, or battlements—can keep lust from penetrating even the thickest walls. Don Pedro Tenorio, immediately take this woman prisoner and bring her to a tower. In secret, have the Duke taken so that he carries out his obligations to her.

ISABELA: Great Sire, turn your face to me!

KING: The offense behind my back, the punishment too. (Exit the King.)
DON PEDRO: Duchess, let us go now.
ISABELA (aside): *My sin I can't excuse, but to lay the blame on the Duke lessens my shame.* (Exeunt Isabela and Don Pedro.)

(Enter Octavio and Ripio, his servant.)

RIPIO: You rise very early this morning.
OCTAVIO: Under soft sheets is no place for the victim of Cupid's dart. Thoughts of Isabela and my concern for her honor are with me every moment.
RIPIO: Pardon me, sir, but your love is a wrongheaded one.
OCTAVIO: What are you saying, idiot?
RIPIO: Simply, that to love as you do makes no sense. Do you want me to go on?
OCTAVIO: Continue.
RIPIO: I will. Isabela, does she love you?
OCTAVIO: Fool, do you doubt this?
RIPIO: No; but, may I ask, you—don't you love her?
OCTAVIO: Yes.
RIPIO: To lose your mind over her when she loves you and you love her is madness. If she didn't love you that's one thing—then flatter her, pursue her, shower her with gifts, and wait for her final surrender. But if you both love one another, tell me, why don't you two just marry?
OCTAVIO: Marriage is the way of the laundress or the kitchen maid, fool.
RIPIO: Are we to scorn the washerwoman washing and scrubbing, and spreading her clothes out to dry, giving of herself? Is there anything more greatly to be praised than giving? And by the way, is Isabela the giving sort?

(Enter a servant.)

SERVANT: The Ambassador of Spain just dismounted. He is in the entrance hall, in a fierce rage, demanding to speak with you; unless I am mistaken, he plans to arrest you.
OCTAVIO: Arrest me! For what reason? Tell him to come in.

(Enter Don Pedro Tenorio and guards.)

DON PEDRO: The tranquil sleeper at this hour must have a pure conscience.

OCTAVIO: The honor of a visit from your Excellency banishes sleep. What can be the reason for your coming?

DON PEDRO: The King has sent me here.

OCTAVIO: It is an honor worth my life that I should come into the King's thoughts. Tell me then, what good fortune or star has guided me so that the King should think of me?

DON PEDRO: Rather, Duke, it is your misfortune. As the King's emissary I come on a mission from him.

OCTAVIO: Marqués, from this I do not fret; just tell me the message I await to hear.

DON PEDRO: I've been sent by the King to arrest you; please do not be riled.

OCTAVIO: Sent by the King to arrest me! Of what am I guilty?

DON PEDRO: You know better than I, but perhaps I am on a fool's errand. Now listen to the cause of the mission: One night while going over some problems of state, so late we could spy the dawn's rays, we heard a woman crying "help," her voice echoing throughout the palace. Alerted by these screams, the King himself discovered Isabela in the arms of a powerful-looking man, for one who would dare such a thing would have to be a monster of some sort. The King ordered them both seized. Alone with the man, I tried to disarm him, when the devil-like creature threw himself over the balcony among the elms so lofty they tower above the lovely palace spires. The Duchess, in the presence of all, claimed that the man who—under the promise of marriage—had his way with her was you.

OCTAVIO: What are you saying?

DON PEDRO: I am saying what everybody already knows: that Isabela in a thousand ways…

OCTAVIO: Stop; I can't bear to hear of her perfidy. But if this is but a ruse, silence would do more harm than the truth. Let this poison drip from the lips to my heart, but all this may be false—a case where the ear conceives some rumor and gives birth through the mouth. (aside) *Can it be true that my beloved Isabela could so fatally forget me? But this must be so, for evil news flies on swift wings, good crawls on wobbly legs. But no, this can't be, let not my heart be troubled; all this is but a fantasy meant to stir up rage and trouble my soul.* Marqués, is it possible Isabela has deceived me and mocked my love for her? Could such a thing be? Oh woman! Honor's terrible law demands I do something, but what is honor to me now? ... Isabela in the palace last night? ... this seems all madness.

DON PEDRO: It is as true as there are birds in the air, true as there are fish in the sea, and true all things are made up of the four elements. As there is joy in glory, loyalty in friendship, betrayal in enmity, darkness in night, and brightness in day, what I say is true.

OCTAVIO: Marqués, I want to believe you, and nothing more could shock me, for, when all is said and done, even the seemingly virtuous woman is, after all, just a woman. There's nothing to do but see it for what it is, since my affront is obvious.

DON PEDRO: Having shown your wisdom and prudence, find the best solution to the problem.

OCTAVIO: To flee is the answer.

DON PEDRO: Then be quick, Duke Octavio.

OCTAVIO: To set sail for Spain is my choice, and there to put an end to my misfortunes.

DON PEDRO: Through the gate of the garden, Duke, you can slip through this net.

OCTAVIO: Oh woman, you are the weakest of reeds, a weathervane that blows with each changing wind. My rage grows and grows. Now, fleeing this deception I seek new lands. My country, farewell. Isabela with another man in the palace.... I feel I may go mad. (Exeunt Octavio and Don Pedro.)

[A fishing village near Tarragona.]

(Enter Tisbea, a young and beautiful fisherwoman, with a fishing pole in her hand.)

TISBEA: I alone of all the girls who stand on the edge of the sea, the waves kissing our rosy feet, am safe from the madness of passion, enjoying a private happiness, free from passion's prison. Here, as the sun's rays spread joy over the sleepy waves, making them sparkle like sapphires, chasing away night's gloomy shadows and transforming the shore's tiny sands into bright pearls and specks of shining gold, I listen to the birds making their plaints of love and the sweet struggle of the waves against the rocks.

With my flimsy fishing pole bent by the gullible fish flopping in the salty sea, or my nets cast, snatching shellfish in their armor-like sides deep down in their watery shelter, I experience great joy, free, safe from the venomous asp of love, which will never sting my heart. Or, sitting in my skiff with my envious companions, I listen and laugh at my companions' laments of hopeless love.

Happy a thousand times am I, for, beneath the roof of straw in my humble hut, love finds no home; my virtue is safe, as if encased in glass, as delicious fruits are conserved in straw. Disdaining the fishermen enchanted by me, I do not listen to their sighs, do not yield to their pleas, do not submit to their offers.

Anfriso, shaped by the powerful hand of heaven, prodigious in body and soul, is possessed of all the graces—measured in words, liberal in works, patient in rejection, silent in suffering. Around my threshold pacing, even in the frosty morn, this hapless lover brightens my shelter with branches of elm. Both the guitar and the shepherd's pipe he plays for me, and to them my ear is deaf. Mine is a world of indifference. I am a stone-like queen. Indeed, I find pleasure in his pain, glory in his infernal desire.

All the women die for Anfriso, but every moment I kill him with my disdain, for it is the condition of passion to love where you find disdain, disdain where you find love, death in happiness, life in contempt. I will not allow my young years to be spoilt by love; for in this carefree period, it is my fortune to be safe from passion's snares. But why bother with such silly thoughts, impeding my labors; let me not be distracted by matters so slight. Let me surrender this pole to the wind, and the bait to the mouth of the fish.

Ah! But two men have thrown themselves into the sea rather than drown as their sail smashes against a reef. Their boat, dashed by the waves lashing its sides, sinks. The sea takes it to itself ... listing, water seeping in the gunwale ... the boat sinks, the sail floating on the surface, driven by the mad wind.

(Off stage): Help, I drown.

TISBEA: One man bears the other who cries "I drown." Admirable gallantry! On his shoulders he carries the other, as Aeneas did Anchises, this sea a second Troy, swimming, bravely cutting through the waves. But on the shore I see no help for them. I'll cry out, "Tirseo, Anfriso, Alfredo!" The fishermen see me. Let's hope they hear me! But, miraculously, these two have made it to land: The one just now swimming breathless, the other with life.

> (Catalinón carries ashore in his arms Don Juan,
> who has fainted, exhausted from saving Catalinón.
> Both men are soaking.)

CATALINÓN: Finally, we reached safety! Damned be the salty sea! If you wish to keep living, keep to the land; out there is madness, forging only death. Where God put together so much water, why couldn't he have made wine instead? Salty water, a fine thing if you're not fishing! If freshwater is not to your taste, what can we expect of salt water? If you could only find a batch of wine, even if a bit warm. If I survive all the water I swallowed, it's no more water for me. From this day I renounce it; even from holy water I'll refrain!

Oh my master, cold and still. Could he be dead now? The sea is the source of this confusion. Damn the first man to take pines to make boats float on the sea and plot the course for fragile timber. Damn those cartographic tailors, who with their astronomical needles sewed lines over the sea, causing this disaster. Damned be Jason!—and his pilot Tifis, too. He's dead. No one will believe me when I say how this happened. Poor Catalinón. What shall I do?

TISBEA: What troubles you?

CATALINÓN: Fisher girl, a surfeit of ills and a shortage of blessings. It looks like my master, to save me, has perished. See if I am right.

TISBEA: No, he is still breathing. Go and call the fishermen in the hut over there.

CATALINÓN: And if I call them, will they come?

TISBEA: They'll come soon enough. Do it right now. Who is this gentleman?

CATALINÓN: The son of the Lord High Chamberlain of the King. And, if he's willing, before the next six days pass, I hope to be a Count.

TISBEA: What is his name?

CATALINÓN: Don Juan Tenorio.

TISBEA: Call my people.

CATALINÓN: I'm off. (Exit Catalinón.)

[*Tisbea rests Don Juan's head in her lap.*]

TISBEA: Dashing youth, excellent young man, noble and handsome fellow, come to.

DON JUAN: Where am I?

TISBEA: You can see for yourself—in the arms of a woman.

DON JUAN: I live in you, even if I die in the sea. Now I have lost every fear, for though the hellish sea may have all but drowned me, it led me to your radiance. A frightful hurricane shattered my boat, throwing me to the feet of one who offers me shelter and a refuge. In the divine sun of your beauty I am reborn, awestruck.

TISBEA: For one so short of breath you have a great deal to say. The sea has put you on the rack: Its cruel waves are painful ropes that have done their job and made you talk. Surely, you must have swallowed much water, for your speech fairly gushes. After your many torments I fear you bring some to me. Oh please do not turn out to be a liar like Odysseus or a Trojan horse washed up on my shore. Though you come soaked to the skin, I sense a fire within you, and if, being wet, you burn, what will you do dry? In you there seems to be the promise of many flames. Please God you do not lie!

DON JUAN: Would that God had drowned me in the silver waves, for alive my senses have perished, smothered by love of you. You are like the sun: You burn all that your snowy white skin touches.

TISBEA: However cold you may be, you contain a flame which sets me afire. Please God you do not lie.

(Enter Catalinón, Coridón, Anfriso, and other fishermen.)

CATALINÓN: Now they're all coming here.

TISBEA: Your master is alive.

DON JUAN: The sight of you restored all my lost breath.

CORIDÓN: What do you want of us?

TISBEA: Coridón, Anfriso, friends...

CORIDÓN: We have often sought in different ways this happy chance. Tell us what you command, Tisbea. As soon as the order issues from your carnation-like lips, to prove our idolatrous love, it will be done, whether the task be on plains or mountains, to plow the sea or lay waste forests, tread on fire or hold back the wind.

TISBEA (aside): *Just yesterday romantic words like these seemed empty flattery, but today I see they can really be true.* Friends, while standing on this rocky cliff fishing, I saw a ship sinking, and, swimming in the waves, two men. Then I spied, battered and lifeless, a drowned gentleman, carried on another's shoulders, escaping the harsh sea's fury. Filled with pity, I called out to all of you, my cries heard by none.
ANFRISO: Surprised we are you ask us for aught, but ready to carry out your pleasure.
TISBEA: Let us take them to my hut, where we can joyfully entertain them and mend their clothes. My father will take pleasure in this task of mercy.
CATALINÓN (aside): *What a beauty!*
DON JUAN (aside): *Listen to what I'm saying.*
CATALINÓN (aside): *I'm listening.*
DON JUAN (aside): *If she asks you who I am, tell her you don't know.*
CATALINÓN (aside): *What exactly would you have me do?*
DON JUAN (aside): *I'm dying for this comely angler. Tonight she must be mine.*
CATALINÓN (aside): *How do you plan to do that?*
DON JUAN (aside): *Come with me and be quiet.*
CORIDÓN: Anfriso, within the hour the fishermen will begin their singing and dancing.
ANFRISO: Off we go, and let's make a lively fete. (Exeunt Anfriso and Coridón.)
DON JUAN: I am lifeless.
TISBEA: Yet you still walk?
DON JUAN: Like a soul in purgatory, I walk, but in pain.
TISBEA: For a suffering soul you talk a good deal.
DON JUAN: And you understand a good deal.
TISBEA: Please God you do not lie. (Exeunt Tisbea and Don Juan.)

[The Alcázar of Seville.]

(Enter Don Gonzalo de Ulloa and the King,
Don Alfonso de Castile.)

KING: Don Gonzalo, do you have children?

DON GONZALO: A beauty, great Sire, in whose glorious face nature spared no efforts.
KING: I wish to find her a suitable match.
DON GONZALO: As Your Sire pleases; I accept for her. But who is to be her husband?
KING: One of Seville, though not in the country at this time. His name is Don Juan Tenorio.
DON GONZALO: I shall bring the news to Doña Ana.
KING: That is well, and return, Gonzalo, with her answer. (Exeunt Don Gonzalo and the King.)

(Enter Don Juan and Catalinón.)

DON JUAN: Prepare the mares; they're our escape from here. While the fishermen celebrate, get them ready, for surely only the swiftness of their hooves can bring this adventure to a happy end.
CATALINÓN: So, you're going to have your way with Tisbea?
DON JUAN: Since such tricks are my nature, why ask?
CATALINÓN: I've always known you are the plague of women.
DON JUAN: I die for Tisbea, for such is her beauty.
CATALINÓN: A generous payment you give for her hospitality.
DON JUAN: Fool, didn't Aeneas do the same to Dido, Queen of Carthage?
CATALINÓN: Men who deceive and cheat women in this way pay for it when they die.
DON JUAN: If that's the case, I have all the time in the world. It's with good reason your name is CAT-alinón, you're as cautious as a cat.
CATALINÓN: You're right about that—as far as shaming women goes, I want to be a cautious cat.
DON JUAN: Just get the horses ready.
CATALINÓN: Poor woman! What generous payment we give for our lodging! (Exit Catalinón.)

(Enter Tisbea.)

TISBEA: Apart from you, I am beside myself.
DON JUAN: You only feign such passion. I do not believe it for a second.
TISBEA: Why?
DON JUAN: Because if you loved me, you'd show your favor to me.

TISBEA: I am yours.

DON JUAN: Then why do we wait, or what is in your mind?

TISBEA: What crosses my mind is this: The notion that my love for you is a punishment for my coldness to others.

DON JUAN: You're everything to me, all I could ever want, even if it costs me my life; for your love it would be a fair payment. Finally, I promise to be your husband.

TISBEA: We are not of the same station.

DON JUAN: Love is a king who makes all equal with his just law—those who sport silk and those who don coarse cloth.

TISBEA: I almost want to believe you, but men are such deceivers.

DON JUAN: Don't you see the effect you have on me? My heart is your prisoner, tangled in the locks of your lovely hair.

TISBEA: I surrender to you, since you give me your word that you will be my husband.

DON JUAN: I swear to you, as I look into those beautiful eyes killing me, that I will be yours.

TISBEA: Remember, my love, that there is a God above, and that we all must die someday.

DON JUAN (aside): *Then I've got all the time in the world.* My simmering-eyed girl, while I live, your slave I will be. Here is my hand and my faith.

TISBEA: And in my payment to you, I will not be scant.

DON JUAN: Nor in mine, as my passion burns with impatience.

TISBEA: Come into the cabin, it will be the bridal bed of our fiery passion. Until it's time, hide in these reeds.

DON JUAN: Where can I come in?

TISBEA: I'll tell you where.

DON JUAN: You bring glory to my soul.

TISBEA: May your words of love be a pledge: If you break it, may God punish you.

DON JUAN (aside): *Then I've got all the time in the world.* (Exeunt Don Juan and Tisbea.)

(Enter Coridón, Anfriso, Belisa, and Musicians.)

CORIDÓN: Heh, call Tisbea and the fellows, too. Let our honored guest see that even in this remote spot we know how to celebrate.

ANFRISO: Tisbea, Usindra, Atandria! (aside) *I've not seen anything so cruel. She scorches the hearts of others, but never herself gets singed.* Before the dance begins, let Tisbea know about it.

BELISA: Let's go call her.

CORIDÓN: Let us go.

BELISA: Now let's go to her hut.

CORIDÓN: Don't you see, she's busy with her lucky guests, men a thousand would envy.

ANFRISO: Tisbea is always the object of envy.

BELISA: Sing something while we're waiting for her to come. We all want to dance.

ANFRISO (aside): *How can anyone calm a restless soul consumed by jealousy?*

(The group sings)

The girl goes out to fish
Spreading her nets;
And, instead of fish,
She catches hearts.

(Enter Tisbea.)

TISBEA: Fire, fire, I am ablaze, my hut burns. Sound the alarm bells, my friends, the tears of my eyes are not enough to douse the flames. My humble hut burns, another Troy is in flames. With no more Troys, love is reduced to burning humble huts. If, with their fierce rage, love's flames can consume adamant stones, they scarcely will spare fragile straw. Fire, fire, lads, lasses, water, water! Love, mercy, for my soul burns. Oh hut, vile instrument of my dishonor and my infamy, a cave of my offenses! Den of thieves, shelter of my sins. Let fall, like stars on its straw roof, burning embers blown by the wind, so that it be turned to ash. My lover, a false guest, has left a woman dishonored! Like a cloud arisen from the sea, he came and smothered my resistance. Fire, fire, fellows, water, water! Love, pity, for my heart is ablaze! I the one who made fools of men, figures of fun, the victimizer now turns victim. The nobleman, proclaiming his faith under the pledge of marriage, profaned my virtue and my bed. He had his way with me, and I gave him two wings to flee, two mares I had bred, with which he played his prank and sped away. Follow him, everybody, follow him. But, no, it's not important if he gets away: Before the King I'll demand vengeance. Fire, fire, fellows, water, water. Love, pity, my soul is ablaze! (Exit Tisbea.)

CORIDÓN: Follow the vile nobleman.

ANFRISO: Sad is he who suffers in silence, but through him her ingratitude is avenged. Let's follow after her. Her desperate state may lead to a worse misfortune.

CORIDÓN: This is how pride ends. Her madness and conceit brought all this about!

TISBEA: (off stage): Fire, Fire!

ANFRISO: Tisbea has thrown herself into the sea!

CORIDÓN: Tisbea, stop, hold!

TISBEA: Fire, fire, lads and lasses, water, water! Love, compassion, for my soul is aflame! Love, forgiveness, for my soul is afire.

ACT II

[The Alcázar of Seville.]

(Enter the King, Don Alfonso and Don Diego Tenorio.)

KING: What are you telling me?

DON DIEGO: Sire, only what is the truth, as this letter from your ambassador my brother makes clear: They found him in the King's own apartments with a beautiful lady of the palace.

KING: Of what rank?

DON DIEGO: My lord, it was the Duchess Isabela.

KING: Isabela?

DON DIEGO: She, no less.

KING: Shocking temerity! And where is he now?

DON DIEGO: Sire, I will not hide the truth from you: Last night he arrived in Seville with a servant.

KING: Tenorio, because of my admiration for you, I'll communicate with the King of Naples immediately: Your son will wed Isabela, and somehow we'll pacify Duke Octavio, the innocent victim here. But, immediately, we'll exile Don Juan.

DON DIEGO: To where, my liege?

KING: Let him leave for Lebrija this evening—and only thanks to his father for that.... His exile from Seville will make clear my anger. But, Don Diego, how can we tell Gonzalo de Ulloa about all this tactfully? The marriage I arranged for his daughter is no longer possible. I must find some way to free him from this insult—give him a post in the palace.

DON DIEGO: Then, my lord, we must also consider how to restore honor to this lady, the daughter of such an important figure.

(Enter a servant.)

SERVANT: A gentleman in travel costume has arrived, Sire, who says he is the Duke Octavio.

KING: The Duke Octavio?

SERVANT: Yes, Sire.

KING: No doubt he's learned of Don Juan's mad folly, and to avenge himself comes to plead to be allowed to challenge him.

DON DIEGO: Great lord, in your heroic hands I rest my life, for that disobedient, reckless youth, that Hector of Seville, as his friends call him, is my very existence: As for his many youthful follies, they will disappear as his reason grows with age. If at all possible, don't permit this duel.

KING: I understand you, Tenorio. You speak like an honorable father. Let the Duke enter.

DON DIEGO: Sire, I fall at your feet. How can I repay such kindness?

(Enter Duke Octavio, in travel dress.)

OCTAVIO: I prostrate myself before you. A pilgrim, a miserable exile who seeks from his Master relief of past injustice.

KING: Duke Octavio...

OCTAVIO: Fleeing the mad folly of a woman and the unthinkable insult of a noble, I bow down to you.

KING: Duke, I know of your innocence. I'll write to the King of Naples to restore you to your former state. If it is his wish and consent, I will arrange a marriage in Seville to one whose beauty will make Isabela, were she an angel, seem ugly. The Comendador of Calatrava, the valiant Gonzalo de Ulloa, whom the Moor flatters and fears, has a daughter whose virtue itself is a dowry and beauty no less than a miracle, a sun that outshines the other stellar beauties in Seville: This is she to whom I would give you as a wife.

OCTAVIO: If it has pleased you, my voyage here has been a success.

KING: Make certain the Duke's stay lacks no comfort.

OCTAVIO: Whoever trusts in you, my Lord, leaves satisfied. (Exeunt the King and Don Diego.)

(Enter Ripio.)

RIPIO: What has taken place?

OCTAVIO: The King graciously listened to my complaint. I spoke to him: He saw me, he honored me. I was Caesar with Caesar: I saw, I struggled, and I conquered. And a while ago from his hand I was proffered a wife; plus, he volunteers to have the decree against me voided.

RIPIO: With good reason in Castile they call him the "Generous One." So, then, he offered you a wife?

OCTAVIO: Yes, my friend, a wife, one from Seville, a city known for its strong, angry men and elegant women, spirited beauties who mask half their faces with their veils as they shield themselves from the sun.

(Enter Don Juan and Catalinón.)

CATALINÓN: Sir, stop, the Duke is here, the besotted dupe of Isabela, wearing horns on his head.

DON JUAN: Follow my lead.

CATALINÓN (aside): *First you betray him, then you pat him on the back.*

DON JUAN: In a flash I left Naples at the call of the King, whose requests are laws; so, Octavio, I did not have time to bid you farewell.

OCTAVIO: No matter, for now, Don Juan, I find myself with you in Seville.

DON JUAN: Who would have thought, Duke, that I'd see you in Seville and have the opportunity to serve you here? Imagine, you leaving all the joys and pleasure of Naples! For Seville, even so fine a city as Naples is worth leaving.

OCTAVIO: If I'd heard this in Naples and not in Seville, I'd burst out laughing. But now that I am here, I see that such praise comes short of the mark. Who is it coming from there? The Marqués de la Mota. Forgive my rudeness, but I must leave now.

DON JUAN: If you need me at your side, my sword is at your disposal.
CATALINÓN (aside): *And he yours! With your name he'll enjoy another woman of good reputation.*
OCTAVIO: I'm pleased we've run into one another.
CATALINÓN: And if Catalinón can be of help, gentlemen, you will always find me at your service.
RIPIO: And where can we find you?
CATALINÓN: At the Small Birds tavern, an excellent spot. (Exeunt Octavio and Ripio.)

(Enter the Marqués de la Mota and a servant.)

MOTA: All day long I've looked for you and not been able to find you. All the time you've been here and your friend has sought you.
DON JUAN: Given my deep feeling for you, your longing is only right.
CATALINÓN (aside): *As long as he can't swindle a girl or some valuable from you, you can trust him; otherwise he is cruel, the Jackal.*
DON JUAN: What's going on in Seville?
MOTA: It is all quite changed.
DON JUAN: Women?
MOTA: Not worth talking about.
DON JUAN: Inés?
MOTA: She's off to Old Town.
DON JUAN: That's a good place for her.
MOTA: It was the passing of years that sent her there.
DON JUAN: She'll die there. And what news of Costanza?
MOTA: It's a shame to see her losing both her hair and her eyebrows. They call her the "Old Portuguese" but she thinks they're saying "Bold Beauty."
DON JUAN: And Teodora?
MOTA: This summer she shook the French Malady by sweating up a river, and now she is once again the sweet innocent thing. Just yesterday this little doll lost a tooth whispering sweet nothings to me.
DON JUAN: And what of Julia of the red light Candilejo Street?
MOTA: She keeps piling on the powder and the makeup.
DON JUAN: She always tried to peddle herself as young stuff.

MOTA: Now she's just another dried-up thing.
DON JUAN: The Cantarranas zone, is that still the spot for the better class of working girls?
MOTA: Most of them, Frogs we call them, are just desperate old sluts.
DON JUAN: And are the two sisters still alive?
MOTA: Yes, they learned everything they know from the ugly old bawd.
DON JUAN: That daughter of Satan. How's the older sister getting on?
MOTA: Blanca, broke as a church mouse; she's loyal to her lover and he takes everything she earns.
DON JUAN: So she's fasting, is that right?
MOTA: Yes, a saintly woman devoted to one man.
DON JUAN: And the other one?
MOTA: She doesn't turn away anything, even leftovers.
DON JUAN: A frugal woman indeed! Marqués, what about pranks on the girls?
MOTA: Don Pedro de Esquivel and I pulled off a really nasty one last night, and tonight we've got two more lined up.
DON JUAN: I'll go with you; I too have to visit the nest of two chicks. And how about the different sort of women, under whose windows you pace back and forth?
MOTA: One keeps me up at night wanting her.
DON JUAN: Isn't it mutual?
MOTA: Yes, she favors me and holds me in her heart.
DON JUAN: Who is she?
MOTA: Doña Ana, my cousin, who has just arrived here.
DON JUAN: Where has she been?
MOTA: In Lisbon, with her father who is in the Embassy.
DON JUAN: Is she beautiful?
MOTA: In the extreme. All the qualities of nature flourish in her.
DON JUAN: So beautiful a woman I would love to see.
MOTA: You would see as great a beauty as there is in the court.
DON JUAN: Then marry this angelic figure.
MOTA: The King has already given her to someone, and nobody knows who he is.
DON JUAN: Does she care for you?

MOTA: Yes, and she writes me.

CATALINÓN (aside): *Don't go on, or Don Juan the Jackal will trick you.*

DON JUAN: How could someone who gets such satisfaction from the love of a woman fear disappointment? Write her, seize her, court her, and let the world go to blazes.

MOTA: Today I await the solution to my dilemma.

DON JUAN: Then seize the day! I'll be here waiting for you.

MOTA: I'll be back. Goodbye.

CATALINÓN (aside to the servant): *And you, too, Sir square or round shape, whatever your name is.*

SERVANT: Goodbye. (Exeunt Mota and the servant.)

DON JUAN: Well, now it's just the two of us left. Follow the Marqués; he's just gone into the palace. (Exit Catalinón.)

(A woman speaks through a grill.)

WOMAN: Psst, who's there?

DON JUAN: Who called?

WOMAN: You seem prudent and polite and his friend, so give the Marqués this note right away. Remember, the peace of mind of a lady depends on it.

DON JUAN: I tell you, as a friend of his and a gentleman, I'll give it to him.

WOMAN: That's all. Stranger, goodbye. (Woman exits.)

DON JUAN: The voice has faded. This seems like enchantment. This note came to me as if carried by the wind, no doubt from the one so praised by the Marqués. What fortune! Seville often calls me Don Juan the Jackal of Women, for my greatest pleasure is to shame a woman, depriving her of her honor. Let's see what is inside it when I open it, now that I'm out of the square. If this leads to another prank ... that's going to give me some fun. Yes, this is hers all right; It's signed Doña Ana. It reads: *"My unloving father secretly pledged me to another, without any chance for me to resist, an act that will bring me to my grave. If, as it seems, my love and passion mean something to you, and if your love was true, show it at this time. So that you may see how much you mean to me, come this night to my door, which at eleven will be open. There your hopes of my love will, my cousin, at last be fulfilled. As a signal to Leono-*

rilla and my other ladies, wear a bright-colored cape. My love, you hold all my trust, goodbye." Unfortunate lover! Have you ever seen anything like it? This prank really makes me laugh. I'll have her, by God! … with the same guile and deception I used on Isabela in Naples.

(Enter Catalinón.)

CATALINÓN: The Marqués is coming now.
DON JUAN: The two of us have something to do tonight.
CATALINÓN: Some new deception?
DON JUAN: A big one.
CATALINÓN: I can't go along with this. All these pranks will end up badly: The sinner sooner or later pays for his sins.
DON JUAN: Fool, have you turned preacher?
CATALINÓN: Right makes one brave.
DON JUAN: And fear the coward. Remember this: He who serves has no will of his own; his is to do, not to tell. A servant is like a gambler: The more he puts in the pot, the greater his winnings.
CATALINÓN: And it's the one who does and says most who's the big loser in the end.
DON JUAN: This time I'm giving you a warning. There won't be a next time.
CATALINÓN: From now on, whatever you ask me to do, I'll do.
DON JUAN: Quiet, here comes the Marqués.
CATALINÓN: Will he be a victim, too?

(Enter the Marqués de la Mota.)

DON JUAN: Without my seeing who, Marqués, a woman, discreetly, through that grating, gave me a message for you. She says that at twelve tonight, go secretly to her door (aside: *which will be open at eleven*), where at last you will enjoy the fruit of your love; and as a sign for Leonorilla and her women, you are to wear a bright-colored cape.
MOTA: What are you saying?
DON JUAN: That someone, I don't know who, gave me this message.
MOTA: All my concerns are fled; now, in their place, serenity. Oh, my friend, it is only through you that my hope is reborn. Let me kiss your feet.

DON JUAN: It is with your cousin, not me, you will find your pleasure.

MOTA: My joy is such I'm near mad. Oh that the sun would hurry and set.

DON JUAN: The sun is already setting.

MOTA: Let's go friends, and return later to change to evening dress. I am mad for joy!

DON JUAN (aside): *Sure you are, but at twelve no doubt you'll be even more delirious.*

MOTA: Oh, my lovely cousin, my cousin in my heart, who will reward my faithful love.

CATALINÓN (aside): *So help me God, I wouldn't give a centimo for your cousin.* (Exit the Marqués.)

(Enter Don Diego.)

DON DIEGO: Don Juan?

CATALINÓN: Your father is calling you.

DON JUAN: What is your command, sir?

DON DIEGO: It is my wish to see you more prudent, more disciplined, and possessed of a more savory reputation. Or do you seek to bring my days to an early end?

DON JUAN: What brings you here to say this?

DON DIEGO: Your way of life and your mad doings. It's come to this: The King has ordered me to expel you from the city; he is justly outraged at a certain misdeed of yours, a crime so shameful I can't bring myself to mention it ... in the Royal Palace, involving a betrayal of a friend. Traitor, may God punish you with suffering equal to your sin ... and though God seems to nod at your sins, your punishment will not be long in coming. And there is punishment for those who swear falsely in his name, for when death comes, He is a harsh judge.

DON JUAN: In death? Then I've got all the time in the world. Between now and then is a long time.

DON DIEGO: It may seem shorter than you think.

DON JUAN: And this exile to please his majesty, will it be long?

DON DIEGO: Until the furor from your treachery and recklessness quiets down—the unjust insult to Octavio has been satisfied and the scandal you've brought to Isabela smoothed over—the King wishes you exiled to Lebrija now, a slight punishment for your wickedness.

CATALINÓN (aside): *If the poor old fellow knew of the fisher girl escapade, he'd be a might angrier.*
DON DIEGO: If you are deaf to counsel, of all I do and all I say, I must leave your punishment to God. (Exit Don Diego.)
CATALINON: The old man was moved.
DON JUAN: Tears come easily to old men. Let's find the Marqués, night has already fallen.
CATALINÓN: Let's go then, so you take pleasure of his beloved.
DON JUAN: This will be a prank to go down in history.
CATALINÓN: I just pray we get out of this in one piece.
DON JUAN: Catalinón, will you cease?
CATALINÓN: You, Master, truly are the jackal of women, always on the prowl. There should be a town crier warning, "Maidens, beware, a man who deceives women is on the loose, the Jackal of Seville."
DON JUAN: You've given me a fine title.

(Enter the Marqués in bright clothing
and musicians singing.)

MUSICIANS: *For the Man who awaits a great pleasure,*
Every minute is an hour...
DON JUAN: What does this mean?
CATALINÓN: It's music.
MOTA: That song seems to be about me.
DON JUAN: Who's there?
MOTA: Is that Don Juan?
DON JUAN: Is that the Marqués?
MOTA: Who else could it be?
DON JUAN: As soon as I saw the cape, I knew it was you.
MOTA (to the singers): Sing, now that Don Juan is here.
MUSICIANS: *For the Man who awaits a great pleasure,*
Every minute is an hour...
DON JUAN: Which is the house you're looking at?
MOTA: That of Don Gonzalo de Ulloa.
DON JUAN: Where shall we go?
MOTA: To Lisbon.

DON JUAN: How, if we're here in Seville?
MOTA: That surprises you? Don't you know the worst street girls of Lisbon live here in the best city in the province of Castile?
DON JUAN: Where do they live?
MOTA: In the Street of the Serpent. There every fallen Adam becomes a lover inhabiting this valley of tears, hoping for a bite of pleasure from one of the many Eves on this street who gladly take his gold.
CATALINÓN: I've no wish to travel through this nasty street at night, for what is at first honey turns into muck. I won't even tell you what got poured on me one night from some window.
DON JUAN: Now on this street I've got a little trick planned for one of the working girls.
MOTA: Near here I've got a hell of a one cooked up, too.
DON JUAN: If you'll allow me, Marqués, I'll show you how these tricks can really turn out well.
MOTA: To better pull this thing off, wear my cape.
DON JUAN: That's fine with me. Come and show me the house.
MOTA: As you're doing this, imitate my voice and speech. See that lattice?
DON JUAN: I see it.
MOTA: Go up to it, say, "Beatriz," and go in.
DON JUAN: What sort of woman can I expect?
MOTA: One pink and cold.
CATALINÓN: Like the clay pots we use to keep water cool.
MOTA: We'll wait for you by the road around the church.
DON JUAN: Goodbye, Marqués. (Exit Marqués.)
CATALINÓN: Where are we going?
DON JUAN: Quiet, stupid, quiet; now I'm off to carry out my prank.
CATALINÓN: Nobody gets away from you.
DON JUAN: Tricks are my great joy.
CATALINÓN: You tossed the cape at the bull.
DON JUAN: No, the bull tossed the cape at me. (Exeunt Don Juan and Catalinón.)
MOTA: The woman will think I'm Don Juan.
MUSICIANS: What a sweet prank.

MOTA: This is to get the right thing through an error.
MUSICIANS: All this world is error.
(They sing) *For the Man who awaits a great pleasure,*
   Every minute is an hour. (Exeunt omnes.)

[The home of Don Gonzalo.]

DOÑA ANA (off stage): Imposter! You're not the Marqués. You've tricked me.
DON JUAN: I say I am.
DOÑA ANA: Cruel enemy! You lie, you lie.
(Don Gonzalo enters with a drawn sword.)
DON GONZALO: That voice is Doña Ana's.
DOÑA ANA (within): Will no one slay this assassin of my honor?
DON GONZALO: Could there be greater boldness? Her honor dead, she cries out, and her voice so clear it might be a bell.
DOÑA ANA: Kill him!

(Enter Don Juan and Catalinón with drawn swords.)

DON JUAN: Who is this here?
DON GONZALO: One whose honor, the fortification of his life, has been crushed, crumbled, fallen to the ground by you, traitor.
DON JUAN: Let me pass.
DON GONZALO: To pass—by the point of my sword.
DON JUAN: Know this means your death.
DON GONZALO: What is my life to me now?
DON JUAN: Realize, then, that I must kill you.
[The two men fight.]
DON GONZALO: Die, treacherous swine!
DON JUAN: This is the way I die.
CATALINÓN (aside): *If we get out of this one, no more pranks, no more goings-on.*
DON GONZALO: Oh. You've slain me.
DON JUAN: You did this to yourself.
DON GONZALO: Without honor, I was already dead.
DON JUAN: Let's flee. (Exeunt Don Juan and Catalinón.)

(Enter Don Gonzalo dying,
and then Mota and the Musicians.)

DON GONZALO: Come back here, this blood only makes my rage burn still hotter.... Alas, I'm a dead man; there's no hope of revenge. My fury will pursue you though, for you're a traitor, and any traitor is nothing but a coward.

[The corpse of Don Gonzalo is carried off stage.]

[The street.]

(Enter Mota and musicians.)

MOTA: Soon it will be midnight, and Don Juan is very late. Waiting is such a burden!

(Enter Don Juan and Catalinón.)

DON JUAN: Marqués?
MOTA: Don Juan?
DON JUAN: It's me. Take your cape.
MOTA: And how did your prank come off?
DON JUAN: Pretty sadly, actually, you might even say deadly.
CATALINÓN: Yes, deadly is the word.
MOTA: You had your prank. Now what shall I do?
CATALINÓN (aside): *The joke's on you!*
DON JUAN: This prank has been a costly one.
MOTA: Don Juan, this woman's ever complaining to me, so this one's on me.
DON JUAN: It's nearly midnight.
MOTA: As my joy is great, I hope morning never comes.
DON JUAN: Goodbye, Marqués.

[Don Juan and Catalinón on another part of the stage.]

CATALINÓN: A hell of a fix this dupe will be in.
DON JUAN: Let's be off.
CATALINÓN: An eagle couldn't catch me. (Exeunt both.)
MOTA (To the musicians): You all can go home now; I'll stay here alone.
A MUSICIAN: God made night for sleeping. (Exeunt the musicians.)

Don Juan: The Jackal of Seville

VOICE (offstage): Have you ever seen such a terrible thing, such a misfortune?

MOTA: Good Lord! I hear voices in the Alcázar Plaza. What could be going on at such an hour? A chill of fear grips me. The huge flames of those torches make it seem another Troy is ablaze, and a whole squadron of them are coming this way.

(Enter Don Diego and the Guard with torches.)

DON DIEGO: Who's there?

MOTA: Somebody waiting to find out the cause of this noise and this disturbance.

DON DIEGO: He's wearing the cape the Comendador told us of with his last words. Arrest him.

MOTA: Arrest me? (He reaches for his sword.)

DON DIEGO: Put the sword back in its scabbard; the bravest act is to avoid resorting to arms.

MOTA: You speak to the Marqués de la Mota in this way?

DON DIEGO: Surrender your sword. The King has ordered your arrest.

MOTA: Good God!

(Enter the King and his attendants.)

KING: Nowhere, nowhere I say, in Spain, not even in Italy, if he goes there, will he escape.

DON DIEGO: Sire, here is the Marqués.

MOTA: Your Majesty has had me arrested?

KING: Take him and have his head put on a pike. You dare stand before me?

MOTA (aside): *Ah! Such is the price of love's tyrannous glory. But the King's wrath shocks and frightens me.* Will I not be told why I am being taken prisoner?

DON DIEGO: Who better would know the cause than you?

MOTA: Me?

DON DIEGO: Let's be off.

MOTA: What a bizarre confusion! (Exit.)

KING: Have the trial arranged for the Marqués immediately, and tomorrow lop off his head. And for the Comendador, let there be a burial according to his rank, in a monument made of bronze and assorted stone, with a relief of the Comendador atop it. Let it boast large letters formed from mosaic pronouncing his certain vengeance. All—burial, bust, and tomb—let them be made at my expense. Where has Doña Ana gone to?

DON DIEGO: To the Queen seeking her protection.

KING: This loss will weigh heavily on all Castile, and bring to tears the Order of Calatrava. (Exeunt omnes.)

[The countryside near the village of Dos Hermanas.]

(Enter Batricio, newlywed husband, with his bride Aminta; Gaseno, her father; Belisa; shepherds, musicians.)

SHEPHERDS singing:
A pretty sight is the April sun that rises
Shining on the clover and mint.
And though like stars,
Still Aminta is more beautiful.

BATRICIO: Over this carpet of flowers, on fields still white with frost, may the sun's first feeble rays beckon and light us as to our wedding bed.

AMINTA: Sing to my beloved sweet words over and over.

The singers:
A pretty sight is the April sun rising
On the clover and mint.
And shining though like stars,
Still Aminta is more beautiful.

GASENO: You've sung well, sweeter than the *Kyrie*.

BATRICIO: With your lovely pink lips you shame even the bright face of the April sun.

AMINTA: Batricio, I thank you, false flatterer that you are; but if I merit the sun's rays, it is because I am your moon. I wax because of your sun's warmth, wane when we are apart. Let the dawn sing to you with a gentle greeting.

The singers:
A pretty sight is the April sun rising
On the clover and mint.
And shining though like stars,
Still Aminta is more beautiful.

(Enter Catalinón in travel garb.)

CATALINÓN: Ladies and gentleman, we seek to join the wedding festivities.

GASENO: The happy news must have spread. Who is it that comes?

CATALINÓN: Don Juan Tenorio.

BELISA: The handsome one.

BATRICIO (aside): *This is a bad omen: A nobleman and a handsome one at that: Now all joy is removed, and in its place there is naught but jealousy.* Who told you two of my wedding?

CATALINÓN: We heard about it on the road to Lebrija.

BATRICIO (aside): *I imagine that the Devil sent him.... But what am I fretting about? Let the whole world come to my wedding. But, of all things, a nobleman ... at my wedding, an evil omen!*

GASENO: Why not invite everybody—The Colossus of Rhodes, the Pope, Prester John, and Don Alonso XI with his court, where they can see examples in Gaseno of spirit and welcome. There are mountains of bread, wine as plentiful as the waters of the river Guadalquivir, towers of bacon and armies of birds, and delicious chickens and doves. That today such a great nobleman should come to the town of Dos Hermanas honors these old white hairs.

BELISA: The son of the High Chamberlain...

BATRICIO (aside): *This is all an evil omen. They'll give him the seat next to my bride. I've yet to enjoy the fruits of my marriage. This cannot be good, and I am damned by the Heavens to jealousy. I must just love, suffer, and be silent.*

(Enter Don Juan Tenorio.)

DON JUAN: Traveling, I chanced to learn of a wedding in this village, and naturally sought to share in the celebration.

GASENO: Your grace's arrival lends the ceremonies honor and status.

BATRICIO (aside): *And what about me? To this I say: "You darken this affair."*

GASENO (to Batricio): Won't you give your place to this nobleman?

DON JUAN: With your permission, I wish to sit here. (He sits next to the bride.)

BATRICIO: If you sit before me, my lord, you'll seem to be the groom.

DON JUAN: I could have done much worse, if I had been.
GASENO: But he is the groom!
DON JUAN: My mistake and ignorance. Please excuse me.
CATALINÓN (aside): *Unlucky groom!*
DON JUAN (aside): *He's angry.*
CATALINÓN (aside): *I see that; but if he must play the role of the bull, it's not surprising he roars. I wouldn't give a cent for his woman or his honor. Poor fellow—you're in the hands of Lucifer himself.*
DON JUAN: How is it that I have been so lucky, my lady? I dearly envy the groom.
AMINTA: You seem to me a great flatterer.
BATRICIO (aside): *I know that the presence of someone so important at a wedding is an evil sign.*
GASENO: Let us now dine. And your lordship will have a chance to rest.

[Don Juan takes the hand of the bride.]

DON JUAN (aside to Aminta): *Why do you hide your hand from me?*
AMINTA (aside to Don Juan): *It's mine, isn't it?*
GASENO: Let's go in to dine.
BELISA: Let's hear some more singing.
DON JUAN (aside to Catalinón): *What do you say to this?*
CATALINÓN (aside): *I fear a thousand deaths from these peasants.*
DON JUAN (aside): *Lovely eyes, white hands, I burn for them.*
CATALINÓN (aside): *Brand her and put her in the corral. With this one, that makes four.*
DON JUAN (aside to Catalinón): *Look out, they're glaring at me.*
BATRICIO (aside): *A nobleman at my wedding, a bad omen!*
GASENO: Sing.
BATRICIO (aside): *I'm dying.*
CATALINÓN (aside): *Sing now, the tears will come later.* (Exeunt omnes.)

ACT III

(Enter Batricio.)

BATRICIO: Jealousy, like a clock, you measure the minutes by each worry, faithfully telling the time not with hours but with torments, wildly striking not with bells but agonizing passions. Jealousy, you turn life into an ugly joke, converting men into fools: Cease your torment, for it is well known that when love gives life, you give death. What do you want of me that you torment me so? I was right when I saw him at my wedding and said, "This is an evil omen." Wasn't it a fine thing, his sitting down to dinner next to my bride and taking the dinner plate right out of my hand? Every time I sought to grab for the plate he pushed my hand aside, saying, "How uncouth, how uncouth!" When I mentioned this to others at the table, they laughed at me and said: "Don't complain; hush, this isn't anything. You've nothing to fear; it must be the custom in the court." Some custom! What gracious behavior! They wouldn't have acted this way in Sodom—somebody but the groom eating with the bride, and the groom going without a meal. And that other trickster, he eats as much as he wants. "Peckish, are you?" he asks. "You really should eat more," and the second I reach for some food he snatches it away from me. I realize now that this has been a great prank, not a wedding party. This can't be tolerated among civilized people. If this keeps up, I'll wager that when dinner is over he'll go to bed with us and say as he points at me, "Uncouth, uncouth." Now he's coming, I can't stand this: I better go hide, but no, I can't, I think he's seen me now.

(Enter Don Juan Tenorio.)

DON JUAN: Batricio.
BATRICIO: Sir, what do you command?
DON JUAN: To let you know...
BATRICIO (aside): *What other reason could he have come for but to make me more miserable?*
DON JUAN: For some time, Batricio, I have loved Aminta and I have...
BATRICIO: Snatched away her honor?
DON JUAN: Yes.
BATRICIO (aside): *This only goes to prove what I already guessed. If she hadn't wanted him here, he'd never have come: After all, she is nothing but a woman.*
DON JUAN: The truth is this: Aminta, jealous or perhaps desperate, thinking I had forgotten her, decided to marry another; so she sent me

a letter telling me to come, and I promised to fulfill our love. Listen to what I say: Think of saving your life, for, without a second thought, I'll kill whoever interferes with my plans.

BATRICIO: If you put your plans in my hands, I promise to assist you in any way, for honor and a woman's name in the mouths of others bring only suffering to a man. A woman on the tongues of others always loses more than she gains. Like bells women are judged by what others hear. It is a received truth, her reputation always suffers when a woman's name rings from a cracked bell. I no longer want her, the light of my love's rays has been darkened: A woman who may be good or may be bad is a coin looked at in a dim light. She's all yours, keep her for a thousand years. Mine is to endure, to know, and to die. (Exit.)

DON JUAN: I vanquished him with his own honor, for peasants always hold tight to their honor, forever seeking to protect what is for them the purest truth. After so much lying and deception and inconstancies it seems honor abandoned the cities, fleeing to the villages. But before doing the damage, I'll seem to repair it. I'll speak to her father to get the nod for my deception. I know how to work this out, hoping to make her mine tonight. The night is passing, and I want to get hold of her father. Stars that shine above me, make my trick a success. And if my only punishment is to come after I'm dead, then I've got all the time in the world. (Exit Don Juan.)

(Enter Aminta and Belisa.)

BELISA: Look now, your husband will be coming. Come, take off your dress.

AMINTA: With all the unhappiness this wedding has brought, I don't know what to feel, Belisa. All day long Batricio has been bathed in melancholy. Everything is confusion and jealousy—what terrible unhappiness. Tell me, what kind of man is this noble who separates me from my husband? The shame of Spain is the noble class. Leave me alone, I'm beside myself; let me alone with my rage. Damn the nobleman who spoils my bliss.

BELISA: Quiet, I think Batricio is coming, for no one treads in the house so firmly but the groom.

AMINTA: Goodbye, Belisa.

BELISA: Let his anger melt in your embraces.

AMINTA: I can only hope to God that my sighs seem to him words of love, my tears caresses. (Exeunt Belisa and Aminta.)

(Enter Don Juan, Catalinón, and Gaseno.)

DON JUAN: Gaseno, may God's blessings fall on you.

GASENO: I'd like to accompany you, so I can give my daughter best wishes on her good fortune.

DON JUAN: There's time for that tomorrow.

GASENO: You're quite right: With all my heart I give you my child. (Exit Gaseno.)

DON JUAN: My wife, you mean. Saddle the mares, Catalinón.

CATALINON: For what time?

DON JUAN: For the dawn, which will roar with laughter at my hoax, then to flee in the morning.

CATALINÓN: In Lebrija, Lord, another wedding awaits us. For the sake of your life, get this over quickly.

DON JUAN: This will be the prank par excellence, the prank of pranks.

CATALINÓN: Let's just hope it comes off with our skins intact.

DON JUAN: My father is the chief justice and a favorite of the King, what can worry you?

CATALINÓN: These higher-ups often get God's punishment. And lookers-on, like me, can end up the big losers in card games.

DON JUAN: Go, saddle up, tomorrow I want to sleep in Seville.

CATALINÓN: In Seville?

DON JUAN: Yes.

CATALINÓN: What are you saying? Look at what you've done. Look how short is even the longest life, and after death there is hell.

DON JUAN: Let there be many deceptions. If death is my only worry, then I've got all the time in the world.

CATALINÓN: Sir...

DON JUAN: Go away, you're annoying me with your foolish worries. (Exit Catalinón.)

DON JUAN: Now that the night is dark and silent, and the Pleiades are emerging, I'll put my plan into practice. Passion alone guides me to my destination, her bed. Aminta!

(Enter Aminta in a nightgown.)

AMINTA: Who calls Aminta? Is that my Batricio?

DON JUAN: I'm not your Batricio.
AMINTA: Then who can you be?
DON JUAN: Look carefully, Aminta, at who it is.
AMINTA: Oh God! I'm lost! In my rooms at such an hour.
DON JUAN: This is my hour.
AMINTA: Go away; I'll scream! Don't abuse the respect you owe my Batricio. Know that even in little Dos Hermanas there are Roman Emilias—and vengeful Lucretias, too.
DON JUAN: Just a few words. And let the precious scarlet in your cheeks descend to your heart.
AMINTA: Go away, my husband will be coming.
DON JUAN: I am your husband. Does this surprise you?
AMINTA: Since when?
DON JUAN: From this moment.
AMINTA: And who arranged this?
DON JUAN: My joy.
AMINTA: And who married us?
DON JUAN: Your eyes.
AMINTA: With what power?
DON JUAN: My sight.
AMINTA: Does Batricio know about this?
DON JUAN: Yes, and he has forgotten you.
AMINTA: Forgotten me?
DON JUAN: Yes, and I adore you.
AMINTA: How?
DON JUAN: With my two arms.
AMINTA: Get away.
DON JUAN: How can I, if I'm dying?
AMINTA: What a lie!
DON JUAN: Aminta, listen and you will know if what I say is true, for women can tell when a man lies. I am a nobleman, heir of the Tenorios, one of the families who settled Seville. After the King, my father is the most revered and esteemed figure in the Court. On his word hangs life and death. Travelling on the road, I chanced to find you, for sometimes love, perhaps unawares, guides things in this way. I saw you, I adored

you, my heart was set afire. My love so moved me, I feel we must be married, matching the deed to the thought. And though the kingdom may grumble about it, the king may oppose it, my father may be angry and try to prevent it, your husband I must be. What is your answer to me?

AMINTA: I don't know what to say. Your true meaning is hidden, encased in pretty phrases. If I am married to Batricio, which it is clear I am, our marriage isn't annulled just because he's changed his mind.

DON JUAN: A marriage, unconsummated because of malice or deceit, can be annulled.

AMINTA: With Batricio everything was a simple truth.

DON JUAN: Now, all you need do is give me your hand and let it pledge your love.

AMINTA: You're not deceiving me?

DON JUAN: I would be the one deceived.

AMINTA: Then swear you'll carry out your promise.

DON JUAN: I swear by the snowy cold hand of yours, which until now has resisted my burning passion, and the infernal fire you stir in me, to carry out my word.

AMINTA: Swear to fulfill your pledge or suffer the curse of God.

DON JUAN: If through deceit I should not do as I have pledged, may I suffer a perfidious death ... (aside) *by some fellow, but not a live one, please God!*

AMINTA: Then with this oath I am your wife.

DON JUAN: My heart I extend to you in my arms.

AMINTA: Yours is my heart and my life.

DON JUAN: Oh, my most precious Aminta. Tomorrow I'll give you silver-buckled shoes with golden studs for your lovely feet, a necklace to wrap around your alabaster throat, and rings set in shiny precious pearls for your fingers.

AMINTA: From today on, my love is yours.

DON JUAN (aside): *How little you know Don Juan, the Jackal of Seville.*

(Exeunt Don Juan and Aminta.)

[In Tarragona.]

(Enter Isabela and Fabio in travel dress.)

ISABELA: It was in the night, mask of the day, dark antipode of the sun, that the pledge was uttered and I robbed of my precious and cherished jewel.

FABIO: It serves no end, Isabela, to bemoan your loss and weep your eyes out. Love is all deception, and scorn always prompts rage; the lover who laughs today soon finds his heart broken. But now observe, the sea is unsettled and the risk of a storm nears. The galleys have taken refuge near the tower that crowns this beach.

ISABELA: Where are we now?

FABIO: In Tarragona, and soon we will be in beautiful Valencia, palace of the sun. Enjoy yourself there a few days, and then on to Seville where you will see the eighth wonder of the world. And consider this: If you lost Octavio, you've gained Don Juan, a nobleman more striking and of more famous lineage. What makes you so sad? It's said that Don Juan is already a count. The King has decided to marry you to him, and his father is a councilor to his Majesty.

ISABELA: The source of my sadness is not my marriage to Don Juan, for everyone knows his rank. That my shame has become a topic of common gossip, that is why I suffer; the general knowledge of my sin will be the source of my tears as long as I live.

FABIO: Over there, Duchess, a simple fisherwoman, sighing tenderly and gently weeping, approaches, clearly is coming to see you. While I summon your people, you two may share a soft lament. (Exit Fabio.)

(Enter Tisbea.)

TISBEA: In waves of Spain's potent sea, a fire of passion emerged, which my scalding tears could not extinguish, transforming my humble cabin into a fiery Troy. Cursed be the wood that made the ship that brought him to me! Cursed be the bitter crystal sea on which he travelled, bringing pain to me as it did to Medea! Cursed be the sails, and the first man to twist the hemp that fashioned the instruments of deception that brought him to me!

ISABELA: What, beautiful fisher girl, is the source of your sweet plaint of the sea?

TISBEA: Yes, true, I cry out to the sea a thousand times. Oh how fortunate are you who may laugh at its torment.

ISABELA: I too make complaints of the sea. Where are you from?

TISBEA: From a hut now whipped by the powerful wind. Beneath its straw roof my heart was adamant as a diamond, only softened by an arrogant monster who emerged from the sea, melting it as the sun's rays do the hardest wax. Your boat is pulled by bulls; are you then another Europa?

ISABELA: Against my will I'm brought to Seville to marry.

TISBEA: If my shame provokes some compassion in you and since the sea has also brought you pain, allow me to follow you as your humble servant. For, if my pain or my shame does not put an end to me, I will petition the King to right a cruel deception, an act of malice done me by Don Juan Tenorio, an exile tossed ashore near dead from drowning. In his perilous hour I provided him shelter and made him a guest; then, like a serpent in a field of grass, with the promise of marriage, he played me for a fool. God help the woman who trusts a man. In the end he left me: Now don't you think I have the right to avenge myself?

ISABELA: Quiet, stupid woman! Get out of my sight, you've been the death of me! But if your pain has provoked you, you're not to blame. Go on with your tale.

TISBEA: If only this were just a tale.

ISABELA: God help the woman who trusts a man! Who will accompany you?

TISBEA: A fisherman, Anfriso, and my poor father, unhappy witness of my suffering.

ISABELA (aside): *There's no vengeance to fit my rage.* Come along with me.

TISBEA: God help the woman who trusts a man! (Exeunt Tisbea and Isabela.)

[In Seville.]

(Enter Don Juan and Catalinón.)

CATALINÓN: Everything has gone to hell!

DON JUAN: What?

CATALINÓN: Octavio has discovered your double dealing in Naples, and Mota, justly enraged, goes around speaking ill of you and that phony message business with the cape switch you used to pull off the seduction which has stained his honor. They say that Isabela's on her way to marry you and...

DON JUAN (slapping him): Quiet!
CATALINÓN: Ouch! You broke a tooth!
DON JUAN: Chatterbox, where did you get all this nonsense?
CATALINÓN: Nonsense! Nonsense! It's the truth!
DON JUAN: I'm not asking you that. Even if Octavio wants to kill me, does that mean I'm dead? Don't I have hands to defend myself? Where are we lodging?
CATALINÓN: On an out-of-the-way street.
DON JUAN: Fine.

[Don Juan and Catalinón are in a church.]

CATALINÓN: Now you're safe in a church; it's a haven for us.
DON JUAN: Tell my enemies to kill me here during the day. Did you see the groom from Dos Hermanas?
CATALINÓN: I saw him—all anxious and sad.
DON JUAN: Two weeks will have passed before Aminta catches onto the gag.
CATALINÓN: She's so far gone she's calling herself Lady Aminta!
DON JUAN: God, that was a good one!
CATALINÓN: A swell one indeed, but it won't last long, and she'll end up in tears.

[They see the tomb of Don Gonzalo de Ulloa.]

DON JUAN: Whose tomb is that?
CATALINÓN: Here Don Gonzalo is buried.
DON JUAN: He's the one I killed. That's a fine tomb they gave him.
CATALINÓN: The King himself ordered it. What does the inscription say?
DON JUAN: "Here, trusting in the Lord, awaiting to avenge a traitor, lies a noble gentleman." That inscription makes me want to laugh ... and you, lifeless statue, will avenge yourself, will you, with your beard of stone?

[Don Juan pulls at the beard of the statue.]

CATALINÓN: You mustn't try to pluck it; such a beard does not bear pulling.
DON JUAN: Cold Stone, this evening at dinner, I await you in my rooms,

there we'll arrange a challenge, if it's vengeance you seek—although it won't be much of a fight if you use a stone sword.
CATALINÓN: Master, night has fallen. Let's return to our rooms.
DON JUAN: This vengeance has been a long time coming. If you really want vengeance, wake up; and if it is my death you're waiting for, you'll be waiting a long time.

[Don Juan and Catalinón in the inn.]

DON JUAN: Did you shut the door?
CATALINÓN: I shut it as you told me to.
DON JUAN: Hey there, bring me my dinner.
SERVANT ONE: Here it is.
DON JUAN: Catalinón, sit down.
CATALINÓN: I prefer eating in a more leisurely way.
DON JUAN: I say sit down.
CATALINÓN: If you say so.

[A loud rap on the door.]

CATALINÓN: That was some knock!
DON JUAN: Someone is calling on us; see who it is.
SERVANT ONE: I'll be right there.
CATALINÓN: And if it's the law?
DON JUAN: If it is, don't worry.

[The servant returns, fleeing something.]

Who is it? Why are you shaking?
CATALINÓN: This doesn't look so good.
DON JUAN: This is making me very angry. Speak. Answer. What have you seen? Did some devil frighten you? Go to the door. Now!
CATALINÓN: Me?
DON JUAN: Yes, you. Get going, move those feet.
CATALINÓN: My grandmother was found dead hanging on a tree, looking like a bunch of grapes, and, since then, they say her soul walks in pain. Such a knock is very disagreeable.
DON JUAN: Go ahead.
CATALINÓN: You know I'm not very brave.

DON JUAN: Go ahead.
CATALINÓN: What a lovely situation!
DON JUAN: Aren't you going?
CATALINÓN: Who has the keys to the door?
SERVANT ONE: It's only closed with the latch.
DON JUAN: What's wrong with you? Why don't you go?
CATALINÓN: I'll do as you say, but what if the women you deceived have come to avenge themselves on us?

> [Catalinón goes to the door, returns running;
> he falls down and then gets up.]

DON JUAN: What is it?
CATALINÓN: Good God! They're killing me, they've got me.
DON JUAN: What's got into you? Who's going to kill you? What have you seen?
CATALINÓN: Sir, I came there ... then I went there. Who grabbed me? Who tried to carry me away? I went to the door, then blind.... When I saw him.... I swear to God! He spoke and said, "Who are you?" An answer came, I answered, then.... I stumbled and I saw...
DON JUAN: Who did you see?
CATALINÓN: I don't know.
DON JUAN: How wine can mix somebody up. Give me the candle, chicken. And I'll see who calls on us.

> [DON JUAN takes the candle and goes to the door, encountering Don Gonzalo head on, looking as he did on his tomb. Don Juan backs up, obviously upset, grasping his sword in one hand, the candle in the other. Don Gonzalo comes towards him, moving slowly, at the same deliberate pace as Don Juan.]

DON JUAN: Who goes there?
DON GONZALO: I do.
DON JUAN: Who are you?
DON GONZALO: I'm the honorable gentleman you've invited to dine with you.
DON JUAN: There will be dinner for two, and anybody else you might want to invite. The table is already set. Sit down.

CATALINÓN: God help me! Saint Panuncio, Saint Anthony. So, dead people eat, do they? By his gestures he says "yes."
DON JUAN: Sit down, Catalinón.
CATALINÓN: No, sir, let's say I feel full already.
DON JUAN: This is absurd—afraid of a dead man. What would you do if he were alive? This is nothing but stupid, peasant fear.
CATALINÓN: Dine with your guest. As for me, I've already eaten.
DON JUAN: Do you want to make me angry? Get over here, I'm waiting.

[The servants begin to quake.]

DON JUAN: And you two, what are you saying? What are you doing? Idiotic trembling!
CATALINÓN: I never cared to dine with someone who comes from distant lands. How could I, Master, dine with a stone guest?
DON JUAN: Stupid cowardice. If he's made of stone, what can he do to you?
CATALINÓN: Leave me with a broken head.
DON JUAN: Speak to him politely.
CATALINÓN (To the statue): How are you getting on? The land in the other world, is it nice, flat, mountainous? Do they give prizes for poetry there?
SERVANT ONE: Nodding, he says "yes" to every question.
CATALINÓN: Over there do you have many taverns? If Noah is there, there must be.
DON JUAN: Enough! Let us have some wine.
CATALINÓN: Sir Dead Man, do they use snow to cool their wine the way they do here?

[The ghost nods his head.]

That's fine, snow; it must be a lovely country.
SERVANT ONE: He said yes.
DON JUAN: If you want some music, they'll sing for you.

[The dead man nods.]

SERVANT TWO: He said yes.
DON JUAN: Sing.
CATALINÓN: Sir Dead Man has good taste.

SERVANT ONE: It's certain he is a noble and a friend of merrymaking.
(Singing offstage):
> *If you wait for my love,*
> *My Lady, my reward in death,*
> *Then I've got all the time in the world.*

CATALINÓN: For sure the heat has put him off his feed, or he's a fellow of tiny appetite. I'm shaking carrying this dish. They're not big drinkers where you're from.

[Catalinón drinks.]

I'll drink for the two of them. A toast in stone, by God! Now I'm a little less shaky.
> *If that time has come,*
> *That I may enjoy,*
> *Then let a long life be mine,*
> *And let life pass by.*
> *If you wait for my love*
> *Then I've got all the time in the world.*

CATALINÓN: Which of the many women you've played false with are they singing about?

DON JUAN: They're all a joke to me right now. In Naples, Isabela...

CATALINÓN: That's no longer a prank, sir, you're to do the right thing and marry her. You tricked the fisher girl who rescued you from the sea, paying back her hospitality in false coin. You tricked Doña Ana...

DON JUAN: Quiet. We have with us one who paid dearly for her and awaits his vengeance.

CATALINÓN: He's a man of some courage; he's made of stone, you of flesh: This isn't going to work out well.

[The ghost indicates that he wishes the table cleared and that he be left alone with Don Juan.]

DON JUAN: Clear the table. By his gestures he's telling us that he wishes to be alone with me, and that everyone else leave.

CATALINÓN: By God, this is bad! Don't stay here, because a dead man can kill a giant with one blow.

DON JUAN: Everyone out! If I were a coward like you.... Go, he approaches.

[They leave the two alone; the ghost gestures
that the door be closed.]

Now the door is shut. I'm waiting. Say, ghost, shadow, or phantom, what is it you want of me? My word I give to carry out your wishes. If you are a soul in pain, or await some act or prayer of mine to bring you everlasting peace, tell me. Are you enjoying God's grace? Did you die in a state of sin? Speak, I am in suspense.

[The ghost speaks slowly, solemnly,
as one from the other world.]

DON GONZALO: You'll carry out your promise to me like a gentleman?
DON JUAN: Honor I possess, and my word I carry out, because I am a gentleman.
DON GONZALO: Give me your hand; do not fear.
DON JUAN: Fear, you say? I, feel fear? If you were hell itself, I'd still give you my hand.

[He gives the ghost his hand.]

DON GONZALO: With this hand and this pledge: Tomorrow at ten I await to dine with you. You will go then?
DON JUAN: I thought you'd ask a greater task. Tomorrow I will be your guest. Where shall I go?
DON GONZALO: To my chapel.
DON JUAN: Shall I go alone?
DON GONZALO: No, the two of you. And keep your word as I have kept mine.
DON JUAN: I say that I will; I am a Tenorio.
DON GONZALO: I am an Ulloa.
DON JUAN: I'll be there without fail.
DON GONZALO: I believe you. Goodbye.

[He goes to the door.]

DON JUAN: Goodbye. Wait, I will bring you light.
DON GONZALO: Do not bother; I am in a state of grace, and have no need of man's lights.

[He exits slowly, step by step, looking at Don Juan,
and Don Juan looking at him, until the ghost
disappears, leaving Don Juan alone and in terror.]

DON JUAN: Good God! My whole body is soaked in sweat, and my heart turned to ice. When he took my hand and squeezed it, I felt as if it were hell itself. Never have I felt such heat. The way he breathed as he spoke each word, it was so cold it too seemed like the breath of hell. But all this is just imagination; fear and the fear of the dead are nothing more than peasant cowardice. If I don't fear a forceful, living noble with faculties and reason and a soul, why fear the dead? Tomorrow I'll be off to his chapel to be his guest, and let all of Seville fear and admire my valor. (Exit.)

(The Alcázar of Seville. Enter the King
and Don Diego Tenorio and those accompanying them.)

KING: Has Isabela at last arrived?
DON DIEGO: Yes, and she is very displeased...
KING: Doesn't she take to the idea of marriage?
DON DIEGO: She feels that she is now the object of scorn.
KING: There's another reason for her anguish. Where is she?
DON DIEGO: She's lodged in the convent of the Discalced Sisters.
KING: Let her leave the convent this second; I want her to take a place, privately, as one of the Queen's ladies here in the palace.
DON DIEGO: If the marriage is to be with Don Juan, my lord, let him come here in your presence.
KING: Let him come and let this be known everywhere: From today on he is Don Juan, Count of Lebrija, with everything attached to that title. If Isabela is worthy of a Duke and has lost one, now she has won a Count.
DON DIEGO: For all your kindness I prostrate myself at your feet.
KING: You indeed deserve my favor; given your many services for me, this falls short of my debt. It seems to me, Don Diego, that today would be a good time to arrange the marriage of Doña Ana.
DON DIEGO: With Octavio?
KING: It is not appropriate that Duke Octavio be the one to restore her honor. Doña Ana, through the Queen, has asked me that I pardon the Marqués; with her father dead, she seeks a husband. If she's lost one,

she's gained another. You and a few others will inconspicuously go immediately to the Fortress of Tirana and fetch her, and, to satisfy her insulted cousin, I will pardon him.

DON DIEGO: What I so long desired now has come to pass.

KING: This very night, you may tell her, the marriage will take place.

DON DIEGO: Everything turns out well in the end. There will be no problem persuading the Marqués.

KING: You may also forewarn Octavio. The Duke has a difficult time of it with women; to him they're naught but opinions and talk. I'm told that he's very angry with Don Juan.

DON DIEGO: I'd not be surprised if he has realized that Don Juan is the cause of so much of his suffering. The Duke is coming.

KING: Don't move from my side, for you are involved in the insult to him.

(Enter Octavio.)

OCTAVIO: I prostrate myself at your feet, mighty King.

KING: Arise, Duke, and cover your head. What is it you ask of me?

OCTAVIO: On my knees I have come to beg a boon, one which deserves to be granted.

KING: Duke, if it is a worthy request, you have my word it will be granted. Ask.

OCTAVIO: You already know, Sire, from your ambassador's letters and what's on the lips of many, that Don Juan, with typical Spanish arrogance, one night, in Naples, a painful one for me, posing as me violated the virtue of a lady.

KING: Don't go on; I learned of your misfortune. What is it you seek?

OCTAVIO: Permission to challenge this traitor on the field of honor.

DON DIEGO: That no! His is the most noble blood…

KING: Don Diego!

DON DIEGO: Sire.

OCTAVIO: Who are you to speak this way in the presence of the King?

DON DIEGO: I am silent because the King demands it; otherwise my sword would offer you an answer.

OCTAVIO: You are an old man.

DON DIEGO: In my youth those in Naples and Milan got some painful lessons from the sword I wielded.

OCTAVIO: But now your blood is cold; "I was" means nothing, only "I am."
DON DIEGO: Then "I was" and "I am."

[He grasps his sword.]

KING: Hold; that is quite enough. Silence, Don Diego. You show little respect for my person. And you, Duke, after the weddings are over, we'll speak at some length. Don Juan is my Chamberlain and a branch of the trunk of the man before you. So show regard for him.
OCTAVIO: I'll do as you command.
KING: Come, Don Diego, with me.
DON DIEGO (aside): *Oh my son, how badly you repay the love I've shown you.*
KING: Duke.
OCTAVIO: Great Sire.
KING: Tomorrow your wedding will take place.
OCTAVIO: It will be done as you please. (Exeunt the King and Don Diego.)

(Enter Gaseno and Aminta.)

GASENO: This gentleman will tell us where to find Tenorio Don Juan. Sir, around here is there a Don Juan, a well-known fellow?
OCTAVIO: I think you must mean Don Juan Tenorio.
AMINTA: Yes, that Don Juan.
OCTAVIO: He's to be found here; what do you want of him?
AMINTA: That gent is my husband.
OCTAVIO: What?
AMINTA: How come someone in the palace here like you didn't know that?
OCTAVIO: Don Juan said nothing to me of this.
GASENO: Could that be?
OCTAVIO: Yes, by God.
GASENO: When they marry, he'll be getting a very upright woman, worthy to be married to anyone. Down to her bones, she is an Old Christian, with not a drop of Jewish blood; and she has some rentable properties of her own, so even a count or a Marqués would be lucky to have her. She wed Don Juan, leaving Batricio for him.
AMINTA: Tell him how I was a virgin before he took me.
GASENO: This is not a courtroom; we're not making a plea.

OCTAVIO (aside): *This is a prank of Don Juan, and to satisfy my vengeance I'll have them tell all this to the King.* What is it you seek?
GASENO: I want either the wedding to take place or to present our complaint to the King.
OCTAVIO: Of course; your intent is a fair one.
GASENO: Reasonable and just.
OCTAVIO (aside): *Unless I'm mistaken, this is my chance.*

[In the Alcázar there is a wedding.]

AMINTA: Oh, mine?
OCTAVIO (aside): *I'll arrange it so that this all works out for me.* Come where you may dress, my lady, in a courtly fashion, and then you'll go with me to the King's apartment.
AMINTA: You will take me by the hand to Don Juan.
OCTAVIO (aside): *This is my little scheme for Don Juan.*
GASENO: This solution is a comfort.
OCTAVIO (aside): *These two will serve to avenge Don Juan and his betrayal of Isabela.* (Exeunt omnes.)

[A street near the church where the Comendador is buried.]

(Enter Don Juan and Catalinón.)

CATALINÓN: How did the King receive you?
DON JUAN: More lovingly than my father.
CATALINÓN: Did you see Isabela?
DON JUAN: Her too.
CATALINÓN: How was she?
DON JUAN: Like an angel.
CATALINÓN: Did she receive you well?
DON JUAN: Her milky-white face was flushed with a pink tone, like a rose at dawn emerging from its green tomb.
CATALINÓN: So, tonight is the wedding.
DON JUAN: For sure.
CATALINÓN: If this had taken place sooner, you wouldn't have tricked all those other women; but you're taking a wife now and this carries with it many responsibilities.

DON JUAN: Have you become a fool?

CATALINÓN: You'd be better off marrying tomorrow; today's Tuesday, a bad luck day.

DON JUAN: That's all nonsense and lies perpetuated by fools. The only bad day is one when I'm without funds; every other's a joy.

CATALINÓN: Let's go; you must change your clothes. They're waiting for you, and it's already late.

DON JUAN: We've got other business to take care of, even if they're waiting.

CATALINÓN: What's that?

DON JUAN: To dine with the dead man.

CATALINÓN: A madness of all madnesses!

DON JUAN: Don't you see? I gave my word.

CATALINÓN: And if you break it, what of it? What's your word to someone made of stone?

DON JUAN: The dead man could call me despicable, without honor.

[They approach a church.]

CATALINÓN: We've come to a church.

DON JUAN: Knock.

CATALINÓN: What's the point of knocking? Who'll answer? The sacristans are asleep.

DON JUAN: Knock at this small door.

CATALINÓN: It's open.

DON JUAN: Go in then.

CATALINÓN: Let the friar go in with a sprinkler and a stole.

DON JUAN: Follow me and be silent.

CATALINÓN: Silent?

DON JUAN: Yes.

CATALINÓN: May the good Lord save me from such invitations. Good God, this is dark for so big a church. Oh my Lord! Hold on to me, someone's grabbing at my cape.

(Don Gonzalo enters.)

[He looks as he did before. He meets them.]

DON JUAN: Who's there?
DON GONZALO: It is I.
CATALINÓN: I'm dead!
DON GONZALO: I'm the dead one; there's nothing to fear. I didn't think that you'd keep your word, since you take so little seriously.
DON JUAN: You think me a coward.
DON GONZALO: Yes, after all, you fled the night you slayed me.
DON JUAN: I fled to protect my identity. Now you have me in front of you; tell me right off what you want of me.
DON GONZALO: I wish to invite you to dine with me.
CATALINÓN: Let's skip dinner, shall we? Everything'd have to be a cold meal, since there doesn't seem to be a kitchen.
DON JUAN: Let us dine.
DON GONZALO: To dine you must lift this tombstone.
DON JUAN: If you want, I'll lift those pillars up.
DON GONZALO: You're very valiant.
DON JUAN: I have spirit and a heart within my body.

[Don Juan lifts the tombstone.]

CATALINÓN: This table is as black as soot. Doesn't anybody in the afterlife ever wash it?
DON GONZALO: Sit down.
DON JUAN: Where?
CATALINÓN: Two pages in black are bringing us chairs.

[Enter two figures in mourning clothes carrying chairs.]

They use mourning fineries here too and Flemish table cloths?
DON GONZALO: Sit.
DON JUAN: Where?
CATALINÓN: I already had a late snack this afternoon.
DON GONZALO: Don't answer back.
CATALINÓN: Me, I didn't say anything. (aside): *God in heaven get me out of here.* What dish is this, sir?
DON GONZALO: This is a plate of scorpions and vipers.
CATALINÓN: A fine dish!

DON GONZALO: These are the delicacies we eat. Won't you have something?
DON JUAN: I'll eat anything you serve me, even all the asps you have in hell.
DON GONZALO: I also want there to be singing for you.
CATALINÓN: What sort of wine do you folks in the other world drink?
DON GONZALO: Taste it.
CATALINÓN: Let's see, gall and vinegar, did I get that right?
DON GONZALO: This wine came right from our winepresses.

(Singing is heard.)

Be warned that all our sins are judged by God,
No matter how long it takes, no debt goes unpaid.
CATALINÓN: This is bad news, by God! I figured out what this tune is about and it's talking about us.
DON JUAN: A feeling of ice penetrates my breast.
While you're in the world,
Never say, I've got all the time in the world,
It won't be long till God demands his debt be paid.
CATALINÓN: What do you put in this stew?
DON GONZALO: Fingernails.
DON JUAN: I've dined now, thank you. Have them clear the table.
DON GONZALO: Give me your hand; don't fear; give it to me.
DON JUAN: What's that you say? Me, fear?

[Don Juan gives him his hand.]

...I'm on fire. Don't burn me with your fire.
DON GONZALO: This is nothing compared to the fire you've been seeking. The wonders of God are, Don Juan, inscrutable; and He wants you to pay for your sins at the hands of a dead man; to pay in this way is the justice of God: Who commits sins pays for them.
DON JUAN: I burn, let me free. With a dagger I will kill you. But, oh! I struggle in vain striking at a phantom with blows in the air. I never violated your daughter; she saw through my trick.
DON GONZALO: That does not matter—your intention was clear.
DON JUAN: Let me call to one who can confess and absolve me.

DON GONZALO: There's no time; you thought of that too late.
DON JUAN: I burn! I burn! I die.

[He falls dead.]

CATALINÓN: Nobody escapes from this; for sure, I will die here to accompany Don Juan.
DON GONZALO: This is the justice of God: "You reap what you sow."

[The tomb sinks with Don Juan and Don Gonzalo. There's a thunderous noise; Catalinón emerges from the ruins of the tomb.]

CATALINÓN: Good Lord! What is this? The whole chapel is aflame, I stayed with Don Juan to keep vigil and watch over him. Dragging myself the best I can, I'll go and tell his father. Saint George, Agnus Dei, let me make it to the street. (Exit.)

[The Alcázar.]

(Enter the King, Don Diego, and those accompanying them.)

DON DIEGO: Sire, the Marqués waits to prostrate himself at your royal feet.
KING: Let him enter then and tell the Count Don Juan, so that he will not have to wait.

(Enter Batricio and Gaseno.)

BATRICIO: Since when, Sire, do you permit those who serve you the gross boldness to offend the less fortunate?
KING: What are you saying?
BATRICIO: That treacherous and detestable Don Juan Tenorio, on the night of my wedding, and before it could be consummated, took my wife from me. And I have witnesses to prove it.

(Enter Tisbea, Isabela, and those accompanying her.)

TISBEA: If Your Highness, my lord, doesn't bring Don Juan Tenorio to justice, as long as I live I shall make my complaint both to men and to God. Exhausted and thrown in the sea, he found life and shelter with me, and he repaid my friendship by lying and deceiving me with the name of husband.

KING: What are you saying?
ISABELA: She is telling the truth.

(Enter Aminta and the Duke Octavio.)

AMINTA: Where is my husband?
KING: Who is that?
AMINTA: Don't you know it yet? The gentleman Don Juan Tenorio, who is going to marry me and restore my honor; and since he's a noble he will not deny me. Order us to be married.

(Enter the Marqués de la Mota.)

MOTA: It is time, great Sire, that the truth be brought to light: You must know that the crime of which you blamed me was Don Juan's, using our friendship to cruelly deceive me, and of this I have two witnesses.
KING: Has there been worse shamelessness? Seize him and kill him immediately!
DON DIEGO: In recompense for my service to you, have him seized and be made to pay for his sins, so that heaven does not throw down rays to punish me for having so evil a son.
KING: This is how my favorites serve me.

(Enter Catalinón.)

CATALINÓN: All here listen, and on my life hear of the most extraordinary event to take place in the world, and after hearing it, slay me. Don Juan, having tricked the Comendador and taken all that is most precious to a man, honor and life, one afternoon pulled on his statue's beard, and, to add to this outrage, invited the statue to sup with him. Oh, that he hadn't! The statue turned the tables and invited him to dine. To be brief, the statue, after many hints at what he was about to do, seized Don Juan's hand, squeezing the life out of him, saying, "God commands I kill you thus, to punish you for your sins. As you sow, so shall you reap."
KING: What are you saying?
CATALINÓN: What is true, saying before he died that his intention to deceive Doña Ana had been found out and foiled.
MOTA: For this news I will richly reward you.

KING: Just punishment of heaven. And now is the time for all to marry, since the cause of all your pain and shame is dead.
OCTAVIO: Since Isabel is a widow, it is my wish to wed her.
MOTA: I with my cousin.
BATRICIO: And we with our women, because now the play is done.
KING: And the tomb of Don Gonzalo will be moved to the great church of San Francisco in Madrid to provide a fitting memorial.

THE END

A Sinner Saved, a Saint Damned
(published 1635)

A Sinner Saved, a Saint Damned, in its portraits of the play's protagonists, Paulo and Enrico, can be read in much the same way *Don Juan: The Jackal of Seville* often is: as a forerunner of psychological drama. For contemporaries, however, the work, like the Don Juan play, was a religious drama, pure and simple. In fact, *A Sinner Saved* is still ranked by many Golden Age scholars as one of the greatest theological plays of the era.

The play was written by Tirso during a time of great religious upheaval. Europe had been roiled by the Protestant Reformation, the Church had responded with the Counter-Reformation, and there was great confusion, concern, and uncertainty over the single most important question for any Christian: "How will I be saved?" This debate was passionate and produced different answers. Some held that we can do nothing on our own behalf because none of us deserve to be saved. God, for reasons we could never know or understand, "elects" some undeserving to be saved and not others. Others maintained that faith alone in the Christian God brings us salvation. Still others asserted that heaven was essentially a meritocracy, and through good deeds we can find a place there. Debates on this critical issue were not just among Protestants or between Protestants and Catholics, but among Catholics themselves, notably the Jesuits and the Dominicans.

A Sinner Saved, a Saint Damned is a play about salvation. Paulo is a pious man who eats grasses, drinks brackish water, and prays constantly. He represents what is usually referred to as Pelagianism: the belief that salvation is attained through good deeds. He makes sacrifices to please God and thinks that is enough. Or, he hopes this is enough. But his fate demonstrates that good deeds are not enough to win God's favor; we must also have faith in Him, which is to say faith in His love, fairness, and mercy—and this Paulo lacks. When his confidence in the eternal efficacy of his good works is shattered by a diabolic deception, he is bereft and falls into the unpardonable sin of Despair—the conviction that no matter what he does, including repent, God will damn him.

Enrico is the diametrical opposite of Paulo: Despite being an inveterate criminal, he is certain he will be saved. Obviously, Enrico does not hold that salvation is based on an accumulation of good works. Rather, he is convinced that, despite his acknowledged unworthiness, God will forgive him because, Enrico believes, God's mercy is unconditional; after his last breath, even without repentance, the Lord will take him up to heaven with Him. This confidence is such that even in the face of death Enrico refuses confession, repentance. His blind trust in divine mercy divorced from any action of repentance is the damnable sin of Presumption. Through his beloved father's persuasion, Enrico in the end does repent and is saved, carried up to heaven by angels.

A Sinner Saved, a Saint Damned dramatizes the need for repentance; that is its clear message. It also demonstrates the importance of love—love of God, love of one another, and the connection between the two. If we do not love God but only view Him as all-powerful, we may come to resent, even hate Him. Arguably, Paulo does hate God, and his self-destructive refusal to repent is a way of getting back at Him.

A Sinner Saved, a Saint Damned
Characters

Paulo: A hermit penitent, later a bandit
Enrico: A criminal
The Devil
Shepherd
Anareto: Aged father of Enrico
Celia: Mistress of Enrico
Lidora: Companion to Celia
Lisandro and Octavio: Visitors of Celia
Pedrisco: A servant of Paulo
Galván: Criminal
Escalante: Criminal
Roldán: Criminal
Cherinos: Criminal
Albano: Old man
Governor of Naples
Warden of a prison
A Judge
Bailiffs
Travelers
Bandits
Prisoners
Jailers
Peasants
Musician

Act I

[A woods with two caves behind.]

PAULO: Bless this isolated, tranquil, solitary refuge, set high up in the mountains. As I leave my cave I see the dawn come over this emerald plain tinged by crystal drops of dew, and, with its hand of pure light, sweep away the shadows of night. Glancing above, I marvel at the sky, the blue carpet on which sit soft clouds, and I long to tear a shred from that azure cover to see the heaven it hides. But from these thoughts I must turn away, for they lead to the road to madness. And, besides, I must remember just one thing: Though I cannot see God, I know that, sitting on His luminous throne, surrounded by an angelic legion, He sees me. Ah, if only in my unworthiness, I could express to Him my infinite thanks for plucking me from the threshold of hell and placing me on the path of virtue, which, followed straight, must lead right to Him.

Listening to the tiny birds chanting their songs as I gaze at these brooks, strips of crystal flowing over fields of green, I ponder this mystery: "If earth offers us such glory, what must be the glory of heaven?" I think of God and His great love for me and cry out, "Lord, be blessed a thousand times for all these gifts and the good You offer me." Here I intend to follow You, never again to be led astray by man's madness, never again opening one of the world's deceiving doors to lose myself in the labyrinth of human folly.

(Paulo goes into his cave. Pedrisco enters from his cave.)

PEDRISCO: Ten years it's been since Paulo took me from my home, marooning me on this mountain, each in his own cave, where we eat only plants and grass. Grass, grass, grass! Carting all this grass down from the mountain you'd think I was a donkey. Munching food nature grew for beasts, day after day, can't turn out well!

Beneath these shady elms, hearing the sweet sound of rushing crystal water, I recite this plaintive verse: "Where can you be, my delicious hams?" When the city, not these crags and boulders, was my haunt, my slightest hunger was a great sadness. But now, my happy moments gone, I guess I'll keep eating greens until one day in May I'll blossom, turning into a meadow. Now Paulo leaves his dark cave, so I'll step into that gloomy one of mine to feast—on my grassy dinner.

A Sinner Saved, a Saint Damned

(Exit Pedrisco. Enter Paulo.)

PAULO: Misery and misfortune! Forced by fatigue to cease my orisons, sleep—that living figure, that frightful image of cruel death—overcame me. A dream I had leaves no doubt I have outraged the Lord, unless perhaps the Enemy of Man has deceived me.

No less a figure than death itself appeared to me. Heavens, if just the vision of death in a dream causes such turmoil, what must it be like at life's end? With his bow—the one that humbles the proud—he shot an arrow in my heart, freeing my spirit from its fleshly prison. My soul then found itself before God's cruel countenance. Next to him the Prosecutor of Souls, one whose fury even in triumph never abates. This frightful figure read out my sins; my good deeds were read by my protecting angel. The weight of my sins raised high the scale, and the Holy Judge damned me to the Den of Dread.

I awoke trembling, tormented, seeing nothing before me but my guilt. I am left in confusion and perplexity, wondering if this is my miserable fate or a trick of Satan. Almighty God, I ask this: Reveal the secret of my eternal end. Lord, the path of virtue I have followed, so leave me not in this perplexity. Am I damned or am I saved? What end is mine? My tears gush from my eyes. Oh tell me, will my end be heaven or hell?

(Enter the Devil from atop a crag.)

DEVIL: Ten years have I tormented this monk with memories and forgotten thoughts, always finding him firm, adamant as a great boulder. Today he doubts his faith, demanding from God Himself the knowledge of his eternal fate. It is his distrust of God that is his sin, his insistence that God Himself reveal such knowledge. The sin this pious man has fallen into is one I know all too well: pride.

Divine license now allows me to tempt him with more deceptions, more temptations. To redeem himself he must battle with might the challenges, the new deceptions I offer him. So, in the form of an angel, I'll give him an answer to his question, one which will cost him his salvation.

(Removing his cloak, the Devil takes the form of an angel.)

PAULO (aside): *The sight of him blinds me. I scarcely can resist my fear.*

DEVIL: God has heard you, has seen your tears.

PAULO: My God, but one question: Will salvation be mine? Shall I ascend to heaven and enjoy Your glory? Your answer ... my only hope.

DEVIL: It is God's command I lead you away from this path of blind confusion, this snare of Man's Foe. To see your certain happiness or sure misery, to Naples you must go. Entering through what is called the Harbor's Gate, you will see—mark me now—right near it, a man...

PAULO: Such contentment your words provide.

DEVIL: ...by the name of Enrico, son of the noble Anareto. By this description you'll know him—handsome, tall—more I do not wish to say, for no sooner will you arrive than you will see him.

PAULO: I'm waiting to know what it is I must ask him when I see him.

DEVIL: There's but one thing you must do.

PAULO: What is that?

DEVIL: Watch him in silence, contemplating his word and deeds.

PAULO: In my blind breast you sow the seeds of chimeras and confusion. I need do no more than this?

DEVIL: To mark this man—that is God's command: Your end is his end.

(He disappears.)

PAULO: Oh mystery supreme! Who will this Enrico be? Already I die to see him. Mine is contentment and joy. No doubt he is some holy man.

(Enter Pedrisco.)

PEDRISCO (aside): *Fortune ever comes to the aid of the most feeble heart. At last, with my stomach full, I am once again myself.*

PAULO: You've come at a good time. We two must make a short journey.

PEDRISCO: I'm hopping and skipping for joy. Where, Paulo, is it to be?

PAULO: To Naples.

PEDRISCO: What am I hearing? Why this trip?

PAULO: On the way you'll learn of a rare experience. Please God it prove a happy one.

PEDRISCO: But what if we are recognized by old friends from there?

PAULO: No one will know us. Changes in our age and dress will be our disguise.

PEDRISCO: It's been ten years we've been away, for sure we're safe now. These days a friend won't recognize you after an hour.

PAULO: Let's go. (aside) *My soul weeps for joy—a joy such as I've never felt. Lord, obedience to You is my sole devotion ... for it is You who send me to see this blessed Enrico who is no doubt a great saint. Lord, I am filled with happiness.*

PEDRISCO: And because I'm going with you, I am, too. (aside) *With this blessing I have a chance to visit Juanilla's Ale House and the Tavern of One Eye.*

(Exeunt Pedrisco and Paulo. Enter the Devil.)

DEVIL: My plan moves apace. Today this doubter will get what he asked for—a vision of his final end.

(Exit the Devil. Enter Octavio and Lisandro.)

[Naples. The home of Celia.]

LISANDRO: The fame of this woman has brought me to her door. She is held the cleverest woman in this kingdom of Naples.

OCTAVIO: That cleverness, however, is the wax of all her vices. She uses it to trick the foolish, to swindle fops, and, with an octave or a sonnet, she drives a thousand men mad. And to seem clever themselves they praise her language, her skill, and conceits.

LISANDRO: Still, I've heard remarkable things about this woman.

OCTAVIO: Did you hear that her house is a brothel whose doors are ever open to the rich Neapolitan, German, Englishman, Hungarian, Armenian, Indian, even to the despised Spaniard, and that her lover is the worst blackguard to walk the streets of Naples?

LISANDRO: You mean Enrico, son of the poor Anareto, bedridden these last four or five years. I've heard about this fellow.

OCTAVIO: This woman gives him all she can. When his vices squeeze him, he comes to her house and beats her, taking away her chains, her rings...

LISANDRO: Poor woman!

OCTAVIO: She has her own crooked ways, filching from novices in love with her their property with her sham poetry.

LISANDRO: Warned by such a good teacher, see if I take your advice.

OCTAVIO: I'll go with you; but my friend, keep an eye on your money.
LISANDRO: We'll go in with some ruse.
OCTAVIO: I'll ask her to write something for a lady. But if Enrico catches us inside we're in serious trouble.
LISANDRO: He's only one man, isn't he?
OCTAVIO: Yes.
LISANDRO: Then I have little to fear.

(Enter Celia and Lidora.)

LISANDRO: By my life, she is beautiful. It's not often so much beauty and intelligence are seen in one woman.
LIDORA: If they can be judged by their appearance, two gentlemen have arrived.
CELIA: What will they want?
LIDORA: The usual thing.
OCTAVIO: She's already seen you.
CELIA: Noble gentlemen, what is it you command?
LISANDRO: We come in boldly, for in the homes of poets and ladies entrance is forbidden to no one.
LIDORA (aside): *What restraint she shows remaining silent after being called a poet.*
LISANDRO: I've been told that yours is an extraordinary cleverness, and that you even exceed in fame Homer and Ovid. So, my friend who praises your skill and I have come in hopes that you'll write something about a certain lady who forgot about my love and married against her will. And, my lady, if my heart is a worthy prize, I'll award it to your beauty.
OCTAVIO: Lady, I came for the same reason. Your skill is a magnet, drawing all those who boast of possessing wit.
CELIA: And who is this to be about?
OCTAVIO: A woman who loved me when she had something to take from me, but now that I am poor has reformed and leads a more virtuous life.
LIDORA (aside): *What a smart thing to do.*
CELIA: You come at a good time. You say that I surpass the fame of Ovid;

well, now I'll do something even he never did: I'll write your letters and another at the same time.
LISANDRO: What cleverness!
OCTAVIO: Wonderful!
LIDORA: Here's ink and paper.

(They sit down at a table. Enter Enrico and Galván, each with a sword and buckler.)

ENRICO: Gentlemen, what do you seek in this house?
LISANDRO: Nothing at all; it was open and we came in.
ENRICO: Do you know who I am?
LISANDRO: We do.
ENRICO: Then get out of here this damned minute. I swear to God, if I get mad ... don't wink at me, Celia.
OCTAVIO: What madness is this?
ENRICO: Though it's far from here, I'll throw you in the sea.
CELIA: My dear, if you love me...
ENRICO: You dare interfere? Move away, or I swear to God I'll slap you.
OCTAVIO: If our presence here disturbs you, we'll both leave.
LISANDRO: Are you a relative or a brother to this lady?
ENRICO: I am the devil.
GALVÁN (aside to Enrico): *I've got the sticker in my hand, let's get them.*
OCTAVIO: Hold it!
CELIA: My darling, for the love of God!
OCTAVIO: We came not with lascivious desires but so some letters might be written.
ENRICO: And you who thinks he's so handsome, don't you know how to write?
OCTAVIO: Cease your anger.
ENRICO: What do you mean "cease"? And what is this business about something being written?
OCTAVIO: Here, take them.

(Enrico tears them.)

ENRICO: Come back for them some other time.

CELIA: You tore them.
ENRICO: That's right, and if I get angry...
CELIA (aside): *Enrico, my darling...*
ENRICO: ...I'll do the same to your faces.
LISANDRO: That's enough.
ENRICO: I must have my way in all things, and, gentlemen, disobey me and count yourselves legless now, for men like you have never posed a threat to me.
LISANDRO: That a man should treat us in such a way!
OCTAVIO: Quiet!
ENRICO: They think they're men, but they have the souls of women. If they wish to be called men of honor, let them defend themselves against this sword.

(Enrico and Galván slash Lisandro and Octavio.)

CELIA: My darling!
ENRICO: Get away!
CELIA: Stop!
ENRICO: Don't anyone try to stop me.
CELIA: What's happening? Oh my God! (Exit Octavio and Lisandro pursued by Enrico and Galván.)
LIDORA: They're running away, isn't this just lovely!

(Re-enter Enrico and Galván.)

GALVÁN: That was some gash I gave him.
ENRICO: Worthless chickens.
CELIA: My darling, what have you done?
ENRICO: Not a thing. How elegantly I put an opening in him, twice the length of your pointer.
LIDORA (aside): *At least no one can say that he goes away from this house empty-handed.*
GALVÁN: I slashed the shorter one and a ton of wool poured out of him.
ENRICO: Celia, you always have to cause me trouble.
CELIA: Calm down, if only for my sake.
ENRICO: Haven't I told you I don't like it when these dandies, all long

curly hair and mustaches, come here? What do you get from them anyway, these curly-haired fops? As far as giving goes, they've got the character of stones, their purses have found their vocation in the Order of Saint Francis. Why let them in? I've warned you about it, but you'll do anything to make me mad.

CELIA: Listen and you'll see that some are not so stingy. I got this chain and ring from them.

ENRICO: Let's have a look. I'll have that chain; it looks like a good one.

CELIA: The chain?

ENRICO: And now I need the ring.

LIDORA: Leave something for the lady.

ENRICO: Don't butt in, she can ask for herself.

GALVÁN: The mouth on this one will get her killed.

LIDORA (aside): *Woe to the woman who loves you, devil's disciple.*

CELIA: All is yours including me. I only ask you to bring us to the Harbor's Gate this afternoon.

ENRICO: You can wear the cloak.

CELIA: I'll arrange dinner for us there. Shall we go veiled?

ENRICO: No, unveiled, I want everyone to know you belong to me. Galván, tell Escalante and Cherinos to go to the Harbor's Gate and wait there with the ladies.

LIDORA (to Celia): *You're so innocent. Have you given him all the jewels?*

CELIA: It's well spent on a man so valiant.

(Enrico and Galván speak apart.)

GALVÁN: Don't forget you were told yesterday you had somebody to kill.

ENRICO: I already spent half the money.

GALVÁN: Then why are you going to the Harbor's Gate?

ENRICO: Galván, let's make plans later. Now, with the rings and chain from Celia, I have all we need. Let the poor fellow live a little while longer; after the chain is spent, we'll deliver our message.

[The Harbor's Gate.]

(Enter Pedrisco and Paulo.)

PEDRISCO: Boy, that's some tale. So you and this Enrico will have the same end.

PAULO: This is the word of an angel: If he's damned, I'm damned; if he's saved, I'm saved. God sometimes works in strange ways.
PEDRISCO: No doubt this Enrico is some saintly fellow.
PAULO: That's my guess, too.
PEDRISCO: This is the Harbor's Gate.
PAULO: Here's where the angel told me to wait for him.
PEDRISCO: This is the place that fat fellow lived, the one who owned the tavern, where I used to drop in. Over there, maybe you remember, that's where that girl who was as tall as a guardsman lived.
PAULO: O vile enemy! Lascivious thoughts begin to plague me. Curse my weak flesh. The Great Enemy holds me fast with memories of past pleasures.

(He throws himself on the ground.)

Tread on me. Step on me again and again.

(Pedrisco steps on him.)

PEDRISCO: Is this what you want? Am I stepping on you the right way?
PAULO: Go ahead. Don't let it pain you.
PEDRISCO: Pain, why should I feel pain? I'll keep it up, but I'm afraid you won't break.
ROLDÁN (offstage): Enrico, stop.
ENRICO (offstage): I'll throw him into the sea. So help me.
PEDRISCO: I heard someone say Enrico.
ENRICO (offstage): What does the world need beggars for?
CELIA (offstage): What are you doing? Stop!
ENRICO (offstage): I'll stop after I throw him into the sea.
CELIA (offstage): What are you doing? Stop!
ENRICO (offstage, to the beggar): I do you a great kindness, removing you from your misery.
ROLDÁN (offstage): What have you done?

(Enter omnes.)

ENRICO: Some beggar came up to me asking for alms. Pained to see him in such misery, and wanting to spare him the shame of begging from someone else, I took him in my hands and flung him in the sea.

PAULO: What a terrible crime!
ENRICO: It was a kindness, now he's no longer poor.
PEDRISCO: It should have been some devil come up to you for alms.
CELIA: Must you always be so cruel?
ENRICO: Don't talk back or I'll do the same to you or anyone else.
ESCALANTE: Let's forget this. Enrico, just sit down.
PAULO: They called that one Enrico.
PEDRISCO: It's got to be another Enrico; this one's already burning in hell's fires. Let's see how this all turns out.
ENRICO: Then everyone sit down. I want to speak to you all. Celia, Lidora, come sit near us with Escalante and Roldán.
PEDRISCO: What a fine bunch of souls, Father. Let's get closer and hear what they're talking about.
PAULO: Still my Enrico hasn't come.
PEDRISCO: Just watch and be quiet before this beast tosses us in the sea because we're poor!
ENRICO: Now I want each of you to tell us about your crimes—thefts, murders, highway robberies, all those sorts of villainies. Whoever has committed the worst deeds will get a laurel crown, placed on him by the rest of us, and then we'll sing him a song of praise.
ESCALANTE: Now you're talking, Enrico.
PAULO: Will God permit this?
ENRICO: We'll start with you, Escalante.
ESCALANTE: I've killed twenty-five poor wretches, broken into six houses, and wounded thirty with my blade.
PEDRISCO: Wouldn't it be sweet to see him cut a caper on the gallows?
ENRICO: Tell us about your adventures, Cherinos.
CHERINOS: First, I stole so many capes I made the merchant who fenced them rich; second, I've stabbed more than a hundred men, though I never killed anyone.
ENRICO: That's all?
CHERINOS: That's all.
PEDRISCO: Suppose the head thief will absolve him?
CELIA: And you, Enrico, what have you done?
ENRICO: Listen, all of you.

ESCALANTE: No lies, right?

ENRICO: You'll hear none here.

GALVÁN: That's the agreement.

PEDRISCO: Father, aren't you listening to these speeches?

PAULO: I'm looking to see if Enrico is coming.

ENRICO: Pay attention now.

CELIA: No one is stopping you.

PEDRISCO: Let's hear the sermon this priest is preaching.

ENRICO: I was born bad, as the course of my life shows. I grew up in comfort in Naples with my father, who I think you all know. Though not a gentleman or of noble blood, he possessed that quality most valued nowadays—wealth. Finally, as I said, I grew up in comfort, but despite my easy childhood I wasn't a stranger to mischief, committing no end of misdeeds as a youth and follies as a young man. From my father I stole, prying open his chests and coffers, filching his clothes, his jewels, and his money. I used everything I stole to gamble, that parent of so many vices. Over and over I would gamble and lose. Penniless, owning nothing, I began my apprenticeship with other artists in the same guild. Before I linked up with them I stole things of little worth, but with my new companions I broke into seven houses, killing their owners and getting my share of the booty to support my gambling. Five of us we were in all. The other four got caught, but nobody fingered me, even under torture.

They paid for their crimes in the town square. After that lesson I did my jobs solo. At night I'd go to gaming houses and wait at the entrance for winners to leave. Ever so politely I'd ask for a tip from their haul, and when they'd reach into their pockets I'd whip out my cruel sword and bury it in their innocent breasts, taking by force what they'd won only to lose. At night I stole capes. With tools to pry open the doors, I made myself the owner of any house. I swindled women, and any woman who didn't fork over money got a face full of scars from my blade.

These were the trifles of my youth. Now listen to my deeds as a man. Befriended only by this sword, the minister of death, I've taken thirty unfortunates from this world, ten for my pleasure, twenty for a doubloon apiece, a bargain price you might say, but on my oath, when I need the cash I'd kill everyone listening to me.

I've raped six virgins, and count myself lucky to have found that many in these loose times. Once, I took a fancy to a woman of lofty state and secretly entered her house to have my way with her. When this lady cried out, her husband rushed to her aid, and a wrestling match ensued between him and me: I got a grip on this man, he lost his balance, and, seeing my chance, I threw him from the balcony to the ground, where he fell dead. His wife began to scream, so I took out my sword and plunged it in her breast five or six times, where rubies of blood poured out of her snow-white flesh, allowing her soul to take flight.

Just for the sake of doing wrong I've sworn false oaths, weaved fantastic stories, schemed and intrigued. A priest once, in righteous zeal, tried to reprimand me—so I struck him so hard he fell to the ground half dead. When a foe of mine was shut up inside an old man's home, I set fire to it, turning everyone trapped inside to ash, even two young brothers.

I never say a word unless it's linked to a curse or an oath or "for Christ's sake," because in that way I know I offend God. I have never attended Mass in my life and, even in danger of death, have refused to confess my sins or appeal to God Almighty. Never do I give alms but instead abuse the poor, as you've just seen. No reverence have I for the Church or its ministers, even stealing chalices and ornaments from altars. Nor do I respect the law, committing a thousand crimes and slaying its ministers. So fierce am I that the law's officers fear to pursue me.

Finally, I am imprisoned by the beautiful eyes of Celia before you here, respected by all for the affection I bear her. When I know she is flush with money she gives me part. Though a small sum, I use it to support my old father, Anareto, who you know. For the five years he has been an invalid, I've kept him in a bed. Such kindness is only fair, since the good old man is poor because of me and my youthful gaming. All I have said to you is true, on my oath. Now it is for you to judge who merits the prize.

PEDRISCO: Upon my soul, Father, his services are so fine he should solicit a place at court.

ESCALANTE: I've got to confess: You deserve the laurels.

ROLDÁN: I agree.

CHERINOS: We're all one on this.

CELIA: The laurels go to Enrico. (They crown him.) Take them, my love, and since dinner awaits, let's be off. Everyone cry, "Hurrah for Enrico!"

GALVÁN: You've done very well for yourself.

CELIA: Everyone say, "Hurrah for Enrico!"

EVERYONE: Hurrah for the son of Anareto!

ENRICO: Let's be off and enjoy ourselves. (Exeunt Enrico and all those within.)

PAULO: Flow tears, flow. Flow swiftly from my breast, do not hold back for shame. Oh how sad this has proven to be.

PEDRISCO: What is wrong, Father?

PAULO: No man is more unhappy. This evil man you just saw, that is Enrico.

PEDRISCO: What's that?

PAULO: Oh, Brother, how grieved and sad am I. This evil man I just saw is Enrico. Yes, Brother, I was told he was the son of Anareto, just like this man.

PEDRISCO: But this one is already roasting in hell's flames.

PAULO: The one thing I feared—how awful is this. God's angel said to me if this man is damned, I am damned; and if he is saved, I am, too. But how could such a man be saved, after so many evil acts—theft, cruelty—and harboring such base thoughts?

PEDRISCO: Who could raise a doubt on that score? He is as sure to go to hell as Judas.

PAULO: Great Lord, Eternal Lord, why inflict this terrible punishment on me? Did I not live in the desert eating bitter grass, drinking brackish waters, only so You, compassionate wise Judge, would pardon my sins? But how different I see it now. I must go to hell ... already their hungry flames scorch my flesh. Oh what cruelty!

PEDRISCO: Show patience, Father.

PAULO: What patience can there be for the damned, for one doomed to hell, that black abyss of never-ending torment? O God! Endless! Endless! Burning! Burning! Always! Oh my God!

PEDRISCO (aside): *Just hearing this scares me.* Father, let's go back to the mountain.

PAULO: We'll return there but not to do unprofitable penance. Knowing that Enrico and I both have the same fate, I'll have his life and his deeds. Is it just that I should live every day a penitent on a hilltop and he a wastrel in the city and at death share a like fate? I'll become one of the bandits in the mountains and match Enrico sin for sin. Before we're damned this world will feel the points of our avenging swords. Who would have thought this could be?

PEDRISCO: That's a smart solution; that's the right thing, Father. Let's get out of here, hang our habits on one of these high trees, and you don a smart outfit.

PAULO: I'll do just that. I'll make the world fear a man who, though just, was condemned to hell. I'll be a bolt of lightning crashing down on the world. Lord, forgive me. My way may seem unjust, but for one already damned, what other justice can there be?

PEDRISCO: But what can we do without money?

PAULO: I'll steal it from the Devil; for sure he has plenty.

PEDRISCO: Let's be off then.

PAULO: Lord, forgive me, if I avenge myself unjustly. You have already damned me and Your word is certain and cannot be revoked. So, this must be the way. I seek a life in this world, since I know a sad end is mine. In the footsteps of Enrico I will walk.

PEDRISCO: I fear I'm already next in line when you get packed off to hell.

ACT II

[On the street; later in the home of Anareto.]

(Enter Enrico and Galván.)

ENRICO: May the devil take gambling!

GALVÁN: You're always unlucky.

ENRICO: Damn these hands, they must be cursed!

GALVÁN: Loaded dice were your downfall.

ENRICO: Loaded or not I never win. This right hand of mine has been my downfall.

GALVÁN: Don't let this make you forget that you're supposed to kill Albano. Lauro's brother already paid you half the fee.

ENRICO: Now that I'm penniless, I'll kill Albano.

GALVÁN: Besides that, there's more business to tend to with Cherinos and Escalante.

ENRICO: I know they're supposed to rob the home of Octavio the Genovese. Don't fret, I'll be the first one up the balcony. In these affairs I always lead the way. Tell them I'm waiting here.

GALVÁN: I'm off like the wind. You never shy from anything. (Exit.)

ENRICO: As they await the descent of the gloom of night, I'll go and visit my aged father enclosed within these walls. Despite my sinful ways I revere him so that I've kept him these five years in an invalid's bed, giving him what I take from Celia and what I get by force, even going without myself. This is the sole virtue in my dissolute life, maintained religiously, the debt the obedient son owes to his father. Now as his end comes nearer, my worry for him grows. Never in my life did I offend him or cause him care. He never learned of my mischief, my youthful follies. Always have I kept him in the dark about my doings, sparing him the heartbreaks I've caused others. Had he learned of my misdeeds, though my insides are more like rock than delicate glass and my heart that of a beast dwelling on a flinty cliff, rather than wound him they would have come to an end.

(He enters the house and draws the curtains of the bedroom. Anareto is asleep in a chair.)

ENRICO: Father.

ANARETO: My beloved Enrico.

ENRICO: Beloved Father, forgive my neglect. Have I been long?

ANARETO: No, son.

ENRICO: I wouldn't wish to cause you bother.

ANARETO: In seeing you I rejoice.

ENRICO: Not even the splendid glory of the sun's pink clouds sweeping away the night's infinite blackness seems so great to the day as you to me. You are the sun, your white hairs giving honor to this kingdom.

ANARETO: You are the crucible where virtue is made pure.

ENRICO: Have you eaten?

ANARETO: My happiness at seeing you took away my hunger.

ENRICO: I'm not reassured by this explanation, since it is born of your great feeling for me. But now it's two o'clock, and you must be hungry. I'll set the table and you must eat. Here in my handkerchief I've brought you something. Please respect my honor for you and eat it.

ANARETO: You must forgive the trouble I cause you.

ENRICO (aside): *With this escudo I kept back from my gambling I brought him something to eat.*

ANARETO: Lord be blessed for giving me a son who would become my arms and legs.

ENRICO: Let me see you eat.

ANARETO: Oh these tired and painful limbs—help me to get up. Your arms infuse strength into me.

ENRICO: In my embraces I seek to give you life, for to be so ill as you is to know death already. Your dinner is ready now.

ANARETO: Not now, my son, sleep has overtaken me.

ENRICO: Then sleep.

ANARETO: Because I am so cruelly abused by this illness, I worry always that each time I see you will be the last ... so, before I die, I would like to see you marry.

ENRICO (aside): *To give him the joy he seeks, I must pretend.* If that is your wish, soon I'll wed.

ANARETO: Then, Enrico, I'll die happy. And seek a woman more virtuous than beautiful, and let her know that she has your trust.

ENRICO: Sleep, the master of the senses, has overcome him. I'll cover him with a blanket. Let him nap.

(Galván enters.)

GALVÁN: Everything is ready. Look [out the window]. Down the street, Albano's coming.

ENRICO: Who?

GALVÁN: Albano—the man you're supposed to kill.

ENRICO: Am I to kill a man for such a trivial reward?

GALVÁN: Are you afraid now?

ENRICO: I have but one fear: that those two eyes now asleep in that house may awaken. Despite my fame I dare not commit a crime where this man sleeps.

GALVÁN: Who is he?

ENRICO: An extraordinary man, the only man I respect or fear, for the wise man thinks his father a great man. Near him I'd never attempt these damnable crimes; his sight alone would hold me back. Just close the curtain and I am cruel once more.

(Galván closes the curtain.)

Now that it's closed, Galván, we can kill every man on earth.

(Galván and Enrico go outside.)

GALVÁN: Look, Albano's coming, the one Lauro's brother wants you to kill.

ENRICO: Since he comes looking for it, consider him dead.

(Enter Albano, an old man.)

ALBANO: Like the years of my life the sun is setting, and my wife will be fretting.

GALVÁN: What's holding you back now, Enrico?

ENRICO: Hand, stay your murderous course. Here I see a man who is a portrait and the living image of him I have always sought to honor. Tell me, if I am cruel now, am I not ungrateful to my father? To kill him would be to kill my father. Today, Albano, my cruel hands grant you the respect your years merit. Though your white hairs are mute, they ask mercy. O white hairs, whoever goes with you goes secure.

GALVÁN: By God, I don't understand you. You are not who you used to be.

ENRICO: Had I known Albano was of such an age, I'd never have promised such a cruel thing.

GALVÁN: Such respect is stupid, useless even. Now, with Albano alive, you'll have to return the money you were paid.

ENRICO: Will I?

GALVÁN: What do you mean, "Will I?"

ENRICO: I will if I wish.

GALVÁN: Here he comes.

(Enter Octavio.)

OCTAVIO: I just ran into Albano, he's alive and well as I am.

ENRICO: Not surprising.

A Sinner Saved, a Saint Damned

OCTAVIO: I thought you'd carry out your word as fully as I gave you the payment. Is this what it means to be a man of your word?

GALVÁN (aside): *He's just asking for it.*

ENRICO: I don't murder old men. If he's insulted you, go this very second and kill him yourself. As for me, I'm content with my payment.

OCTAVIO: Give me back the money.

ENRICO: I'm off now, don't anger me or I swear…

(They struggle.)

OCTAVIO: I'll have my money.

ENRICO: Not from me.

(Enrico wounds Octavio.)

OCTAVIO: You've slain me.

ENRICO: You should regret your folly now. It's arrogant men like you I kill, not old men whose white hairs subdue even titanic spirits. And if you'd like to put this to a test, have God give you another life and I'll kill you again.

GOVERNOR (off stage): Catch him. Kill that man!

GALVÁN: This is bad. More than a hundred men come with the Governor to take you prisoner.

ENRICO: Let six times a hundred come, and if I'm caught my death is certain. If I fight I might just survive; most important, I seek to die with honor and fame. Cowards, come and get me!

GALVÁN: We are surrounded on every side.

ENRICO: Let them come. I'll cut a swatch right through them.

GALVÁN: I'm right behind you.

(Enter the Governor and those with him, and they are attacked by Enrico and Galván.)

GOVERNOR: Are you the devil?

ENRICO: Just a man who flees death.

GOVERNOR: Then give up.

ENRICO: You'll have to take me.

(Enrico stabs the Governor.)

GOVERNOR: My God, I'm slain.
A BAILIFF: He's killed the Governor.

(Men carrying the Governor retreat.)

ENRICO: And though the earth were to open up and bury me, I could not escape my foes. I must throw myself into the sea, sword between my teeth. Its angry center will be my tomb. Almighty God, have mercy on my soul. Though I am the worst sinner, I have never forgotten my faith. Oh, my father, I would be to you as Aeneas to Anchises. Forgive me, father, though I do not carry you in my arms I have you in my heart. How it grieves me to leave you! (Exeunt Enrico and Galván.)

(Enter Paulo and Pedrisco dressed as bandits, with other bandits and three prisoners.)

BANDIT ONE: Since we are all bound to you, brave Paulo, we await your word whether these men live or die.
PAULO: What money did they give you?
PEDRISCO: Not a centime; we had to take it from them.
PAULO: Then what's holding you back, fool?
PRISONER ONE: Pity! Have pity on us!
PAULO: Hang them from that oak.
THE THREE TRAVELERS: Please!
PEDRISCO: Get moving. You three will make a special fruit for all those birds of prey in these lonely woods.
PAULO: Does my cruelty surprise you?
PEDRISCO: Nothing surprises me anymore. To think, a short time back you fasted with such zeal, prayed endlessly, rapturously pleaded with the Divine for the courage to persevere in your penance, and now— the violent captain of an outlaw band, hidden away in these woods, killing travelers after taking their money—what more could be imagined? After all this, there are no more surprises.
PAULO: I compete and will outdo Enrico in cruelty. If I offend the Lord, may He forgive me, but if Enrico and I must end the same, it's just that we live the same.
PEDRISCO: It's too late to give you advice now.
PAULO: Once saintly, I adored God. But then an angel fractured the crys-

talline globe separating heaven and earth to declare to me my foul reward, driving me from virtue's path. Today let heaven decide if I'm the equal of Enrico in evil acts.

PEDRISCO: You poor man.

PAULO: Now flames pour out of my eyes. Today the beasts dwelling on Naples' mounts and the surrounding plains will see a heart more proud than Phaeton's. The trees that surround us will be outraged as day after day I hang a head on each limb, giving these fruits to the birds of prey.

PEDRISCO: You're off to hell in a grand fashion.

PAULO: Go off and hang them right now from an oak tree.

PEDRISCO: Right away.

PRISONER ONE: But sir…

PAULO: Silence, unless you want a still crueler punishment.

PEDRISCO: Come you three.

PRISONER TWO: Oh my God!

PEDRISCO: Fortune makes me the executioner here, so when they come for me I can give the hangman a lesson. (Exeunt Pedrisco and the prisoners and all the bandits but two.)

PAULO (to himself): Since Enrico and I share a way of life, we shall be companions off to hell. I follow your tracks; so when the Eternal Judge damns us, at least we'll have given Him good reason.

A VOICE (singing off stage):
Let no one,
not the worst sinner,
doubt that mercy
which is God's glory.

PAULO: What voice is that singing?

BANDIT ONE: The many oaks prevent us from knowing where the voice comes from.

THE VOICE (still singing):
To gain God's forgiveness
let the sinner approach with firm resolution to repent.

PAULO: You two climb the mountain and see who is singing that ballad.

BANDIT TWO: We'll go and see.

THE VOICE (singing):

*The Supreme Majesty
asks but that the sinner come and ask Him
for that which no one is denied.*

(Enter a young shepherd, tying a crown of flowers.)

PAULO: Come down here, young shepherd. I was confused by your words and their tone just now. Who taught you that ballad? Frightened, I listened to what seemed my innermost thoughts.

SHEPHERD: Sir, the ballad I sang was taught me by God.

PAULO: God?

SHEPHERD: Rather His Spouse, the Church, to whom He gave His power in the world.

PAULO: You said that well.

SHEPHERD: Bear in mind, though I am just a rustic shepherd, my belief in God is firmly rooted. And I know all the Ten Commandments, the precepts God gave us.

PAULO: And could God forgive even a man who has offended Him with acts and with words, thoughts, and deeds?

SHEPHERD: But of course—even if he had more sins than there are atoms in the sun, stars in the sky, rays from the moon, or fish in the depths of the salty sea. His mercy is such that by repeating "I sinned, I sinned" to our Lord several times, the sinner will be received by Him into His loving arms. This is the way of the Lord. Were it not like this, God would not have created such imperfect creatures. What glory would there be if we had been made perfect? He made us weak but offered us His mercy, without which few would enter His kingdom. God is merciful and values the worst sinner, because all of us cost Him sweat and blood and were the reason He spent nine months in the womb of that woman who deserved to be called virgin as a mother—she who conceived as the bright sunlight goes through glass without breaking it. He made His body like a sea, lovingly separated into five bloody rivers. And think of all the sinners who became saints—Peter, Matthew, Francis, and Magdalene, the public sinner. I could give you a thousand examples, but I must return to tend my flock.

PAULO: Stop, shepherd.

SHEPHERD: Stop I cannot, for I walk these valleys lovingly searching for a lost lamb fled from his flock. This crown you see me making with such love is for him if he's found. All this I do at the command of my master who values him highly and paid dearly for him.

(He begins singing again.)

He who has offended God,
let him ask forgiveness,
for the Lord's compassion is denied no one.

PAULO: Shepherd, wait. Stop, or I'll hold you by force.

SHEPHERD: I cannot stop and you cannot stop me, any more than you could halt the course of the sun. (Exit.)

PAULO: In a wondrous way, not human but divine, the shepherd warns me that God is displeased I should doubt His mercy. He promised God will forgive if I but repent, but would not that be so of Enrico, too? I begin to feel I've been in error. But how could the worst man who ever lived be forgiven by God? Why did the shepherd flee, leaving me in such confusion? Oh, if Enrico showed even a flicker of repentance! No, there can be no help for it, no hope: The two of us must be damned.

(Enter Pedrisco.)

PEDRISCO: Paulo, listen and believe the unbelievable: On the green shore, the refuge of so many wild beasts, where the crystal sea pulsates as the anxious cliff awaits its tremendous blow, Celio and I heard a voice that left us half-distracted, crying "I'm drowning!" The sea, as always before a storm, was roaring, eager to swallow two men, thirsty for their blood. Up and down they bobbed, one second seeming fixed to the stars, another plunging to the sea's center. In the crystal waters the heads of these two unfortunates were visible; the waves seemed to be the scaffolds of executioners. At last they landed on the shore. But to get to the point: One of them is Enrico.

PAULO: That can't be.

PEDRISCO: But it is. This is what I've come to tell you, and I'm not blind.

PAULO: You saw him.

PEDRISCO: I saw him.

PAULO: What did he do getting out of the water?

PEDRISCO: He gave out with a "God damn it!" and "Oh Hell!" Some thanks he gives God for saving him.

PAULO (aside): *Yet the shepherd would say the Lord forgives him! I don't know what to believe. But since he turned up here, I will put him to a test.*
PEDRISCO: Your squad is bringing him now.
PAULO: Listen to what you must do.

(He speaks apart with Pedrisco.)

(Enter Enrico and Galván wet, their hands bound, led by bandits.)

ENRICO: Where are you bringing me like this?
BANDIT ONE: The captain is here; he'll give you the answer.
PAULO (aside to Pedrisco): *Do that.*
PEDRISCO (aside to Paulo): *Everything will be done.* (Exit Paulo.)
BANDIT TWO: Is the Captain going someplace?
PEDRISCO: Yes, and you gentlemen, trying to walk on water, where were you off to?
ENRICO: To hell.
PEDRISCO: Why tire yourselves out so, when there are plenty of devils glad to carry you there?
ENRICO: To be less beholden to them.
PEDRISCO: A wise decision not to be beholden to the devil for a thing he does for his own profit. What's your name?
ENRICO: They call me the devil.
PEDRISCO: And to put hell's fire out, you threw yourself in the sea. Where are you from?
ENRICO: If I weren't worn out from struggling with the water and wind and hadn't thrown my sword in the sea, I'd soon enough answer your stupid questions with the edge of my blade.
PEDRISCO: Don't be so vexed, tossing challenges around. Know that I can put a hundred holes in you and that I am as valiant as Hector. He may have killed many men, but I've extinguished many hungers, lamps, fleas, too, just with my touch. Now we'll tie you to a tree.
ENRICO: I'm not stopping you. Do as you will with me. Must I put up with this and not avenge myself?
PEDRISCO (pointing at Galván): And him, too.
GALVÁN: Now my time is up.

PEDRISCO: If your deeds match your face, you've had some nasty life.

(Enrico and later Galván are tied to a tree.)

ENRICO: My heart burns with rage that my power should be so subdued.

PEDRISCO: Let's tie both of them up, that's the Captain's orders. Get over here. I'll blindfold these two with sashes and then we can drive a dozen or so arrows through each of them and save the hangman a task. Tie and blindfold them and put two dozen arrows in each of them. (aside to the other bandits) *This is all a trick; nobody harm them.* (The bandits move away.)

GALVÁN: Show some mercy.

ENRICO: Let them shoot. I'll show no weakness. Heaven takes its just vengeance on me. Now, when I want to repent, I can't.

(Exit Pedrisco and other bandits.
Enter Paulo dressed as a hermit, with a cross and rosary.)

PAULO (aside): *With this ruse I'll test him and see if he remembers God.*

ENRICO: That a man should lose his life unseen, unheard.... My heart rages in its powerlessness. Ah, fortune, in all things you are a miser.

GALVÁN: Every fly that passes by seems like an arrow!

ENRICO: That I should be powerless to struggle against this fate!

PAULO: Praised be the Lord!

ENRICO: May He forever be praised!

PAULO: Learn to bear this angry blow of fortune with fortitude.

ENRICO: Who are you to speak to me this way?

PAULO: A monk who dwells in the desert where you wait for death. You know of course that those men who have tied you to these trees plan to shoot you, so I entreated them to let me speak to you.

ENRICO: For what?

PAULO: So that you might confess, and, in that way, follow the path of God.

ENRICO: Then you can go right on back to where you came from, Father, or whatever you are.

PAULO: What are you saying? Aren't you a Christian?

ENRICO: Yes, I am.

PAULO: No, not if you don't accept the last blessing I offer.

ENRICO: I don't feel like it.

PAULO (aside): *The very thing I dreaded!* Don't you see ... these men are going to kill you.

ENRICO: Keep quiet, will you, brother, and leave me here and let these fellows kill me.

PAULO (aside): *What confusion holds my soul?*

ENRICO: I give satisfaction to no one.

PAULO: You do to God.

ENRICO: If God knows I'm such a great sinner, what's the point?

PAULO: Blasphemy! So that in His sacred love He can forgive you when you die.

ENRICO: Father, what I've never done before I won't do now.

PAULO: Your heart is made of stone.

ENRICO: Galván, what do you think Celia is up to now?

GALVÁN: In this spot who can remember anything?

PAULO: Don't think about such things.

ENRICO: Father, you're starting to annoy me.

PAULO: These holy words, they offend you.

ENRICO: This is very tiresome; if I weren't tied up you'd be in the sea with a kick.

PAULO: Don't you understand, they're going to take your life.

ENRICO: I'm already tired of waiting.

GALVÁN: Father, listen to my confession.

(Paulo removes the blindfolds.
Enter men with crossbows and muskets.)

PAULO: Look over at those men. They've come to kill you.

ENRICO: What's holding them back?

PEDRISCO: Now that you know what your end is, why don't you confess?

ENRICO: I don't want to.

PEDRISCO (to a bandit): Lay one across his chest.

PAULO: This is just desperation. Let me talk to him.

PEDRISCO: Let's get it over with and kill him.

A Sinner Saved, a Saint Damned

PAULO: Stop! (aside) *What grief is this for me! If he is damned, what hope is there for me?*

ENRICO: Cowards, get on with it, open up a door in my chest.

PEDRISCO: This time, do it!

PAULO: Harm him and my confusion will only grow. Remember, my son, you are a sinner.

ENRICO: The worst in the world, and I know it.

PAULO: I seek only what is good for you. Confess.

ENRICO: I don't want to, tedious preacher.

PAULO: Then let pour forth from my breast a river of overflowing tears to drown my soul, for now my trust in God is washed away. Let this coarse cloth drop from my body, for such a costume ill suits such tainted flesh. (He removes the hermit garb.) Like the evil serpent I slide along on my evil deeds; I'm worse in fact than the lowly snake, for he sheds the bad while I the good, accepting my unhappy end.

(He hangs his habit on a tree.)

I hang this sackcloth here and let it say, "Paulo hung me here, for he was unworthy." My baleful destiny I will not oppose; I must exchange the cloth of Christ for the rags of Satan. Give me the dagger and the sword; you keep the cross, for the blood of Christ can no longer wash away my sins. Untie them.

(Enrico and Galván are untied.)

ENRICO: Free, I cannot believe what I have seen. Tell me the truth.

PAULO: Poor wretch that I am! Enrico, oh, that you had never been born, that your mother never brought you to see the light, that your wet nurse had crushed you in her arms, that a lion had rent you to pieces, that a bear had torn to shreds your tender limbs, that you had fallen from the tallest ledge—any of these calamities, rather than you cut short the thread of my hope.

ENRICO: I am thunderstruck.

PAULO: I am Paulo, a hermit who for ten lived years in the wilderness. One day an angel came to me and told me to go to Naples and observe you, for the two of us would enjoy the same eternal destiny. After seeing the sort of man you are, I threw off the sackcloth and became a bandit.

Here I tried testing you to see if in the face of death you would confess.

ENRICO: God puts words in the mouths of angels that man does not always understand, and it may be that you damn yourself by your decision to surrender your hermit's sackcloth. Your lack of trust in God, your vengeance on Him, may be the real cause of your damnation; that He does not unsheathe His justice-wielding sword against you tells me He seeks your salvation. Though the worst sinner that ever walked the earth, one who, even in the face of death, did not repent, I believe I will be saved, not of course from my own deserts, but my trust in God's compassion. I have confidence that His profound compassion will overcome His sacred justice.

PAULO: You've consoled me somewhat.

GALVÁN: By God, I am astounded by all this.

ENRICO (aside): *Oh Father, my beloved Father.* Paulo, I must return to Naples for a precious jewel there. Even if I perish in the quest, I must return there and fetch it. Have one of your men accompany me.

PAULO: Have Pedrisco go, he's bold.

PEDRISCO: Though I hoped he'd choose me, I fear if I go there I may pay for the crimes of my comrades.

ENRICO (to Paulo): Goodbye, my friend.

PAULO: Just the sound of that word makes me want to embrace you.

ENRICO: Though evil, I trust in God.

PAULO: With so many sins, I can't.

ENRICO: Your despair will damn you.

PAULO: I am already damned. Oh, Enrico, that you were never born.

ENRICO: God will pity me.

ACT III

[A cell with bars in the rear through which the street is seen. Pedrisco and Enrico are prisoners.]

PEDRISCO: What a mess we're in now!

ENRICO: What the devil are you moaning about?

PEDRISCO: What the devil am I moaning about? Can't I moan about paying for someone else's crimes? Everybody knows that whoever sins gets punished, but I haven't done anything, so why should I suffer?

ENRICO: Why don't you quiet down? Can't you take it like me?

PEDRISCO: I'll be silent, but I'm hungry and hunger can make even the dead speak and a criminal confess.

ENRICO: You don't think you'll get out of jail?

PEDRISCO: Oh, we'll get out of jail all right … from the start I thought we'd get out of here…

ENRICO: Then what are you going on about?

PEDRISCO: …to be hanged, unless God helps us.

ENRICO: Don't be afraid.

PEDRISCO: All right, but in my heart I think we're going to be dancing with our feet in the air.

ENRICO: We'll have better luck than that.

(Enter Celia and Lidora, stopping in front of the jail.)

ENRICO: Quiet. That's Celia…

PEDRISCO: Who?

ENRICO: …a woman who loves me more than herself. My problem is solved. Do you have something to put the money in she'll have for us?

PEDRISCO: Still my hunger keeps calling me, but I've got a sack for what she brings.

ENRICO: That's too small.

PEDRISCO: I'm beginning to think that the two of us are crazy—you for asking and me for giving it to you.

(They see Celia.)

ENRICO: Celia, my beautiful darling.

CELIA (aside to Lidora): *My God, I'm lost! That's Enrico who called.*

(Approaching the jail window) Señor Enrico.

PEDRISCO: Señor? I don't like the sound of that.

ENRICO: I knew I could trust you.

CELIA: How are you, Enrico?

ENRICO: Fine, and better now that, at the cost of a thousand sighs, my eyes are meeting yours.

CELIA: I want to give you…
PEDRISCO: Now it's come! Oh beautiful woman! What lovely words. Wait a moment while I arrange the money sack.
ENRICO: Celia, what is it you have for me?
PEDRISCO: Lucky man!
CELIA: The news that at nine o'clock tomorrow you'll be hanged.
PEDRISCO: The sack's full now, it won't hold any more.
ENRICO: That I should have to hear such a thing. Celia, listen…
CELIA: I'm married now.
ENRICO: Married, my God!
PEDRISCO: Hold on.
ENRICO: What more can there be? To who?
CELIA: Lisardo. And we're happy together.
ENRICO: I'll kill him.
CELIA: Put away such thoughts and make peace with your Creator.
LIDORA: Celia, let's go now!
ENRICO: I'm losing my mind. Celia, consider…
CELIA: I must rush away.
PEDRISCO: By heaven, I could split a gut.
CELIA: I know what it is you want to tell me—have a Mass said for your soul. I promise I will. May God go with you.
ENRICO: Oh, if only I could break these bars.
LIDORA: That's enough of his laments; let's leave now.
ENRICO: Can there be greater suffering than to have to endure this?
PEDRISCO: You know, this bag is weighing me down.
CELIA: What rage! (Exeunt Celia and Lidora.)
ENRICO: How blind I've been! Is any woman as loose as this one?
PEDRISCO: There's something wrong here, these coins in this bag … they're light as straw.
ENRICO: Good God! Must I put up with such insults? Why can't I break these irons and uproot these bars?
PEDRISCO: Stop this!
ENRICO: Get away from me, fool. By God I must break these chains, my rage cannot be contained.

PEDRISCO: The jailers are coming.

(Enter jailers.)

JAILER ONE: The murdering thief has lost his mind.
ENRICO: I'll not die without some revenge. I'll make a sword from my chain.

(Enrico breaks the chain holding him
and rushes after the jailers and the other prisoners.)

PEDRISCO: Stop, I beg you.
JAILER ONE: Seize him, kill him.
ENRICO: Base prisoners, now you'll see the force jealousy provokes in a desperate breast.

(The jailers and the prisoners flee. Enrico pursues them.)

JAILER TWO: A link got me and knocked me to the ground.
ENRICO: Cowards, why do you run away?
PEDRISCO: A jailer is dead!
VOICES (off stage): Kill him!
ENRICO: What does it mean to kill? Lacking a good sword, this chain will have to do to avenge my insults. Why do you all flee?
PEDRISCO: All this confusion and clamor have brought the Warden.

(Enter the Warden with others. They seize Enrico.)

WARDEN: What's happening here?
JAILER ONE: That thief has killed Fidelio.
WARDEN: Oh my God! If I didn't know that tomorrow you'll hang and provide a public lesson, I'd cut a thousand mouths in your treacherous breast.
ENRICO: God, must I endure this? Despicable Warden, don't deceive yourself and think your rank means a thing to me. I could tear you into two thousand pieces with my bare hands, tear your body to shreds, eat them in mouthfuls, and still that would not be enough to avenge my insults.
WARDEN: Tomorrow at ten you'll find the hangman more valiant than all your words. Put another chain on him and toss him in the dungeon.

ENRICO: That's only right. An enemy of God must not see His heavens.

(Enrico is taken away.)

PEDRISCO: Poor unfortunate Enrico.

JAILER ONE: Not so unfortunate as the dead man; that cruel rap from the chain split his head and spilled his brains on the floor.

JAILER (off stage): Come and get your meal.

PEDRISCO: Just in time. When they string me up tomorrow, I'll have a full rucksack of vittles to share with the devils in hell.

(Exit Pedrisco. Enter Enrico.)

ENRICO: Now, in this blackest of moments, is the time to show the valor for which you are famous.

A VOICE (off stage): Enrico.

ENRICO: Who calls? This voice makes me shudder, and my hairs stand on end. Where is my courage now, the remembrance of my past deeds?

VOICE: Enrico.

ENRICO: It continues to call. My soul is weighed down. Whose voice is that, what is it that makes my heart so fearful?

VOICE: Enrico.

ENRICO: It won't stop and it makes me wonder at my own fear. It comes from over here; maybe it's a prisoner lashed to the chain. Poor wretch.

(Enter the Devil. He is invisible to Enrico.)

DEVIL: I lament your doleful misfortune.

ENRICO: In this abyss of confusion I don't know myself, and I can't stop my heart from hammering with fear. Enrico, where is your courage? Again that clamor.

DEVIL: I've come to free you.

ENRICO: How can I believe such a thing? I don't know who or where you are.

DEVIL: Now you see me.

(The Devil appears in the form of a shadow.)

ENRICO: No more do I wish to see you.

DEVIL: Do not fear.

ENRICO: A cold sweat is spreading over my whole body. Don't come nearer.

DEVIL: Today a new fame will be yours.

(At a signal an opening appears in the wall.)

DEVIL: Do you see that opening? Leap through it and you'll be free.

ENRICO: Who are you?

DEVIL: A prisoner like you, one who seeks to set you free. Now jump immediately.

ENRICO: What shall I do? Of course, I'll free myself, the fear of death urges me on. I'll do it now ... but there's another voice.

VOICE off stage (singing):
Hold that violent step.
Escape is not what you seek,
For you're better off here.

ENRICO: This voice tells me to stay; it says that to stay here will prove the better fate.

DEVIL: That's just an illusion, the product of your fear. Only a madman would fear a happy chance.

ENRICO: You're right, if I stay I'll die.

VOICE:
Hold back, deceived Enrico,
don't flee, to leave is to die,
To stay to live.

ENRICO: The voice tells me that to leave is to die, to stay is to live.

DEVIL: Then, finally, you wish to stay. Your fear has blinded you, but stay a prisoner and you'll see that it will prove a sad ending for you.

ENRICO: Yes, it's better to remain.

(The Devil disappears.)

Now this specter has gone and left me in perplexity. Isn't this the opening? But where is it? Was I blind or did I see a hole there? But I can leave, but how ... for I must die! The voice inspired me with terror. I couldn't feel this fear unless some great harm is to come. I'm prepared for whatever misfortune comes.

(The Warden enters.)

WARDEN: Only I am to go in; the rest stay behind. Enrico!
ENRICO: What do you want of me now?
WARDEN: In the harshest trials courage surfaces; now you must demonstrate yours. (aside) *Even now his countenance doesn't change.* (He reads) "The Attorney General of His Majesty condemns Enrico, the incorrigible criminal and murderer, to be taken from the prison and be brought to the public square and, with a rope around the neck, be hanged on the gallows until he is dead."
ENRICO: Can I really be hearing this? I'd break you into...
WARDEN: Arrogance will gain you nothing. Now is the time to make peace with God.

(Exit the Warden.)

ENRICO: Now I'm sentenced to death and my miserable life has but two hours to run. Oh Voice, the fault is yours. You said that to stay was to live. With good reason I blame you for the death that is soon to come when I could have saved myself.

(Enter a jailer.)

JAILER: Two Franciscan friars are waiting outside to hear your confession.
ENRICO: That's a pleasant joke! Tell those priests to go back to the monasteries, unless they want to taste these irons.
JAILER: But you are about to die.
ENRICO: And I'll do it without confession, and I'll outdo everyone even in my suffering.
JAILER: A heathen could not be worse.
ENRICO: I won't say it again. If I get mad, the marks of this chain will make a tattoo on you.
JAILER: This is enough for me. I'm getting out of here. (Jailer exits.)
ENRICO: Now that my last trial has come, what account can I give to God? Must I confess? But who could remember so many ancient sins, all those offenses I committed against Him? Better forget all that. After all, God is great in His compassion. I praise His mercy and I will be saved by it.

(Enter Pedrisco.)

PEDRISCO: Remember, you're about to die, and those priests are already tired of waiting.

ENRICO: Did I tell them to wait?

PEDRISCO: Don't you believe in God?

ENRICO: I swear I think I'm going to vent my troubles on you and those priests. What do you want with me, devils?

PEDRISCO: ...more like angels, trying to save you.

ENRICO: Keep it up and I'll send you out of this cell with a kick.

PEDRISCO: Thanks for the warning.

ENRICO: Get out and stop bothering me.

PEDRISCO: Well, you're bound for hell, that's for sure. (Exit Pedrisco.)

ENRICO: Oh Voice, hearing you has brought me only harm. Did some enemy send you to avenge himself on me this way? You said to save my life stay in this prison. But soon they're to take me out and hang me. You were false, but I too was at fault: I could have left and saved myself, but stayed out of fear. Somber Shadow, you told the truth; you were on my side. Return and you'll see how my haughty breast flees this dark gloom at the sound of your tremendous voice. I hear people. My end is near.

(Enter Anareto and a jailer.)

JAILER: Speak to him; perhaps your white hairs may pierce so hard a diamond.

ANARETO: Enrico, beloved son, despite my distress at seeing you like this, I rejoice that your sins will be wiped away. Fortunate is the man who, with unswerving repentance, pays for his sins in this life, for this is but a sketch of hell's pains. Dragging myself on this staff, I left my bed to come here, for you are the thing for which I keep myself alive.

ENRICO: Oh, my Father.

ANARETO: Don't be shocked when I say this, but don't dare address me that way.

ENRICO: Does a father speak like this?

ANARETO: A son who turns his back on God has no right to such a name.

ENRICO: Father, can you really be saying such a thing?

ANARETO: If you reject my faith, you are no longer my son. Now the two of us are alone.

ENRICO: I don't understand these words.

ANARETO: Enrico, let me correct your insane thinking. Let your death, which is certain, be my instrument. Today they will hang you, and yet you don't want to make a confession. You think that since the evil is yours, the suffering must be too. Hell is made for such presumption. To avenge yourself in this way is for the hand to strike a rock—when the hand hits it, it is the hand that suffers. When a man flings a stone aloft to trouble heaven, it lands on him.

Today you must die: Know that your fate is sealed. Confess your sins to God, and once they are forgiven, what is death will be life. To be my son, do as I bid you. If not—and how it pains me to say this—no longer call yourself my son, nor will I know you.

ENRICO: Beloved Father, no more! As God is my witness, my soul grieves more at your suffering than at the unhappy fate that awaits me. As a demonstration of my faith, I will confess my sins and humble myself before everyone. That you should command it is enough, my beloved Father.

ANARETO: Then you will be my son once again.

ENRICO: I couldn't bear to give you pain.

ANARETO: Let us go then, so that you may confess, my dear son.

ENRICO: Oh how it grieves me to leave you.

ANARETO: And I from you. Let us go now, my son, so that you may confess.

ENRICO: Oh, how I regret leaving you.

ANARETO: Oh, how I regret leaving you.

ENRICO: Oh, how these eyes of mine long for the light they are to lose.

ANARETO: Let us go, my son. What misery I feel!

ENRICO: Compassionate and eternal Lord, who walks over a path of stars, hear my plea. I've been the most evil of men who ever saw the light of day, one who counts more sins than there are grains of sand beneath the sea. But Lord, Your compassion is still greater: You let Yourself be nailed to the cross to redeem the world for Adam's sin. May I be worthy to reach out and touch but one drop of Your royal blood. Aurora of the heavens, beautiful Virgin surrounded by angels, refuge of sinners, pray for me. Remind your Son of His pilgrimage in this world. Tell Him that now, my spirit illumined, I would endure a thousand deaths before I would give Him offense.

ANARETO: We must hurry inside.

ENRICO: Good Lord, mercy! I cannot say more.

ANARETO: That a father should witness such a thing.

ENRICO (aside): *Now the enigma of the shadow and the Voice is clear.*

ANARETO: Son, let us go.

ENRICO: Who can hear the word and not let a sea of tears pour forth from his eyes. My Father, do not go away, not until my last breath.

ANARETO: Have no fear. May God grant you His blessing.

ENRICO: He will. Being about to die, I know that He is a sea of mercy.

ANARETO: Courage.

ENRICO: I trust in God. Let us proceed to where those who will take away my life await.

(Exeunt Enrico and Anareto. Enter Paulo.)

PAULO: Tired of running through this dense mountain, my men behind me, I'll rest a bit here beneath this willow tree. Oh gentle waters, flowing over tiny pebbles, murmuring, cheering plants and birds with your fleeting din, bring me some happiness now, infuse some mirth into my soul with your chilly current and sonorous voice. You pleasing little birds, who idly warble among the rushes and sages, lighten my grave cares and soften the doleful events of my life with the gentle accents and sweet sounds which issue from your beaks. On this green carpet washed by crystal streams, I seek some distraction from the misfortunes my sad end promises.

(Paulo lies down to sleep and the shepherd boy enters, undoing the crown of flowers he was tying earlier.)

SHEPHERD: Thick wood, green groves of poplar, I return to you once more to look at the forest and to tread the valleys which have proved so costly to me. In a happier time, I was sent by my master to stand guard on your shores over the innocent lambs with their white coats, strips of silver, on a lush green cloth. Once I was held in his immense love because I brought these lambs, white puffs of snow, to him. But since the day his favorite strayed from the flock, I drown in my own tears, my happy songs turned to mournful dirges. To gain this sheep's love, I wove this garland, but, deceived and foolish, he fled the one who steadfastly loved him. Now, unwanted by him, this garland must for the sake of justice be undone.

PAULO: Shepherd, once before I saw you in these mountains, but, then, though not happy, you were less sad.

SHEPHERD: Oh lost sheep! You flee from such glory and attach yourself to such evil.

PAULO: Isn't that the garland you were weaving with such care in the forest?

SHEPHERD: It's the very one, but the foolish sheep would not return to the blessings awaiting him, so I must undo it.

PAULO: If by chance, shepherd, he should return, would you welcome him?

SHEPHERD: Though angry myself, it is my task to open wide my arms to him should he return. My master in his mercy tells me that even if a sheep once white returns to the flock black, I must embrace him and warmly praise him for his return. But, blinded, he will not. Calling with whistles to him in these rugged mountains, walking through briar patches in dense woods in search of him, my feet bleeding from sharp thorns, I can do no more. (Weeping) I must abandon my search and return with this sad news to my master. He'll chide me and say, "Is this the way you guard the sheep I entrust to you?," and I will have no answer for him.

PAULO: If he is your master, you must obey him. (aside) *The shepherd's lovely cheeks are bathed in tender tears*. Since he's abandoned you, dismiss him from your mind and weep no more.

SHEPHERD: This I must do and spread these lovely flowers over the land from whence they came. Farewell my mountains, deserts, and woods. (Exit.)

PAULO (waking up): This dream seems like a tale of my life. The shepherd's words are a puzzle; his words promise a dark enigma. But what light is this that puts to shame the rays of the sun?

(Music is heard and two angels carry Enrico's soul to heaven.)

I can hear heavenly music and two angels seem to be carrying a soul in glory to that sphere above. A thousand times happy is that soul, for today it arrives where it will harvest its joyous fruits. Heaven now opens its celestial curtains. Emerging through these dense clouds you rise, happy soul, to enjoy the heavens, strolling among the paths of joy. Pity any soul denied this reward.

(Enter Galván.)

GALVÁN: Know, famed Paulo, that a large squadron with arms descends the mountain to take us prisoner. You can make them out with their kettle drum and banner. Unless you seek death, we must flee.

PAULO: Who has brought them?

GALVÁN: Those peasants so abused by us on this secluded mountain have gathered together.

PAULO: Then kill them.

GALVÁN: What! You plan to wait for them?

PAULO: Have you no regard for me?

GALVÁN: But our peril is clear.

PAULO: Realize that one worthy man is the match of a thousand peasants.

GALVÁN: Don't you hear the drum banging?

ENRICO: Attack them and fear no injury.

(Enter the Judge with two armed peasants.)

JUDGE: Now you'll pay for your evil acts in these mountains.

PAULO: My breast is ablaze with anger. In acts of cruelty I am Enrico.

PEASANT (off stage): Heh, thieves, give up.

GALVÁN: We'd be better off dead, but I'll flee.

(Galván flees pursued by several peasants.
Paulo enters flailing at the rest. Exeunt all.)

PAULO (off stage): You harass me with your arrows and fight me with every advantage, coming with two hundred to search for twenty.

JUDGE (off stage): He's starting to run over the mountain.

(Enter Paulo slipping, bleeding.)

PAULO: My hands and feet fail me. These peasants have slain me. My cowardice enrages me, I'll go back and kill them.... But I can't. What misery! Thus is Heaven avenged.

(Enter Pedrisco.)

PEDRISCO (without seeing Paulo): Not finding me guilty of Enrico's crimes, they tossed me out the door as soon as they hanged him, and I came back here. But what is happening ... the woods are all stirred up, two peasants are running with swords in their hands, Fineo over there is wounded, Celio and Fabio are running away. Here—oh what great misfortune—the mighty Paulo is outstretched.

PAULO: Peasants, have you come back? I have my sword in my hand, not yet dead, though weak.

PEDRISCO: Paulo, friend, it's Pedrisco.

PAULO: Come to my arms. My God, the peasants have killed me. Now dying, I seek to learn the end of Enrico.

PEDRISCO: They hanged him in Naples' plaza.

PAULO: Can anyone doubt then that he's now in hell?

PEDRISCO: Careful what you say, Paulo, for he died a Christian death, with confession and communion, clasping a crucifix upon which he fixed his gaze. Gentle tears pouring down his face, he begged forgiveness, astonishing all those present. As he died, divine music resounded in the pure air. More miraculous still, two winged angels carried his soul to heaven.

PAULO: Enrico, the most evil man ever reared?

PEDRISCO: Dear God, listen to reason.

PAULO: I die.

PEDRISCO: Consider that Enrico enjoys God: Ask God's forgiveness.

PAULO: How can He give it to a man who's sinned as I have? What you saw must have been an illusion, another man's soul rose to heaven.

PEDRISCO: How can you doubt it? He forgave Enrico, didn't He?

PAULO: God is compassionate.

PEDRISCO: That's very clear.

PAULO: But not with such men. Now I die. Give me your arms.

PEDRISCO: Try to have his end.

PAULO: God gave me His word: If Enrico is saved, I can expect to be saved too. (He dies.)

PEDRISCO: The poor wretch is dead, his body full of wounds. Their fates were exchanged: the sinner Enrico saved, the saint Paulo damned, for his despair. I'll cut some willow branches and cover up his unhappy body. But who is that coming?

(Enter the Judge, Galván, and some peasants.)

JUDGE: We can't have been diligent if their captain has escaped.

PEASANT: I saw him fall, slipping from the highest rocks, pierced by a thousand arrows.

JUDGE: There's a man here.

PEDRISCO (aside): *Oh poor Pedrisco, this time you'll get a beating.*

PEASANT (pointing to Galván): This is Paulo's aide, and accomplice in his crimes.

GALVÁN: You lie like a peasant. I was only the aide of Enrico, who now enjoys the sight of God.

PEDRISCO (aside to Galván): *Galván, brother, don't put the finger on me here, for the love of God.*

JUDGE (to Galván): If you tell us where the captain has hidden himself, I'll let you go.

PEDRISCO: It's useless to search for him when he's dead.

JUDGE: Dead?

PEDRISCO: As I passed by, I found him in this very spot, sir, dying, pierced by many arrows and spears.

JUDGE: And where is he?

PEDRISCO: I put him among these branches. (As he begins moving the branches Paulo appears, bathed in flames.)

JUDGE: What a sight, one to cause horror.

PAULO: If you are searching for Paulo, now you may see him, his body girded by fire and ringed with serpents. I blame no one for these torments, only myself, for I was the cause of my suffering. When I asked God to reveal my divine fate, I offended Him, and that offense was spied by Man's Enemy, who incited me with illusions. Taking the form of an angel, he deceived me. Yet despite his deceptions, I could have saved myself, but I lacked faith in God's compassion. Today when I came to His judgment, He said to me, "Down, accursed of My Father, down to the center of the dark abyss, where you must grieve and suffer." Cursed be my parents for giving me life. And may I be cursed for distrusting God. (He vanishes.)

JUDGE: Mysterious are the ways of God.

GALVÁN: Poor unhappy Paulo.

PEDRISCO: And Enrico is happy, enjoying the sight of God.

JUDGE: Having taken the warning, you are both free.

PEDRISCO: May you live a thousand years! Galván, now that we're freed, what are your plans for the days to come?

GALVÁN: I shall become a saint.

PEDRISCO: I don't see you performing any miracles.

GALVÁN: Have hope in God.

PEDRISCO: Friend, let anyone who lacks faith in God look at this play and learn from it.

THE END

The Timid Young Man at the Palace Gate
(published 1606)

The Timid Young Man at the Palace Gate, composed around 1606, is probably the earliest of Tirso's plays. Generically it is called a *comedia de enredo*, a play of complication. The play is certainly complicated. It contains a plethora of love plots that unfold in a mind-spinning romantic jumble. Character after character is smitten: Mireno, the timid young man of the title, with Madalena, one of the daughters within the ducal palace gate; Madalena with Mireno; the Count Vasconcelos with Madalena; the Count of Estremoz with Madalena's sister, Serafina; Leonela with the Count of Estremoz; Juana, lady-in-waiting to Serafina (seemingly) with Serafina; Don Antonio, cousin of Juana, with Serafina; Serafina with herself; the peasant woman Melisa with Tarso, sidekick of Mireno. Woven into this erotic patchwork pattern are traditional elements found in comedies of the period: characters in disguise, transvestism, impersonations, love at first sight, jealous rivals, and a happy ending with multiple marriages.

Despite its comic and conventional character, *The Timid Young Man at the Palace Gate* has a serious theme: Unbridled sexual expression is a threat to the stability of hierarchical, patriarchal society. This theme is present from the first scene, in which a murder plot is hatched by the Duke's secretary, Ruy Lorenzo, to punish the Count of Estremoz for seducing Lorenzo's sister, Leonela. Significantly, sexual passion prevents the murder from being carried out: The mistress of the would-be assassin teases the plan out of him and then betrays him.

The destabilizing effects of erotic passion extend beyond the palace retinue to the family of the Duke. Before falling in love, his daughter Madalena is the picture of filial subjection. She says to her father: "My will is a wax for Your Grace to imprint on it the stamp which he finds most suitable. For me there is but silence and obedience." She submits without question or complaint to his selection of a husband for her. Once infected by passion, her subservience ends. Ignoring the Duke's choice, she pursues the stranger Mireno, who has been brought to the palace under arrest: After arranging for his release, she makes him her tutor and eventually invites him to sleep with her. Her sister, Serafina, after her passion is ignited from looking at what appears to be a picture of a man (actually herself in male clothing), also rejects her father's choice for her husband and arranges an assignation with the imposter claiming to be the man in the painting.

Serafina's imposter lover is Don Antonio, a high-ranking nobleman. His reaction to Serafina establishes that passion can move men as well as women to ignore their social roles. Impassioned by Serafina after seeing her only once, to be near her he reneges on an obligation to return to his king and assumes a false name and the socially lower identity of secretary to her father. He then spies, Peeping Tom–like, on Serafina; finally, he deceives her into having sex with him by impersonating the "man" she has fallen in love with.

After showing us the tension between sexual desire and social order in *The Timid Young Man at the Palace Gate,* Tirso shows us how this society copes with it: marriage. The couples at the end of the play all wed: the seducer, the Count of Estremoz, with the woman he abandoned, Leonela; the cynical impersonator Antonio with his narcissist victim Serafina; a peasant woman Melisa with the man who rejected her, Tarso (the sidekick of Mireno); and Mireno with Madalena.

Of the four couples, three are joined by either compulsion or bribery; only Mireno and Madalena are linked by love. But, whether one couple love each other, all do, or none is utterly beside the point. Tirso here and in other plays ending in multiple weddings offers a simple, decidedly unromantic message: Marriage is not to make two people happy, it is to contain sexuality in a safe (to patriarchal, hierarchical society), expressible context, such that the dangerous passions it provokes can be avoided or smoothed over.

The Timid Young Man at the Palace Gate
Characters

Duke of Avero	**Ruy Lorenzo**
Don Duarte, Count of Estremoz	**Doña Madalena**
Don Antonio	**Doña Juana**

The Timid Young Man at the Palace Gate

Bato: Shepherd
Vasco: Lackey
Figueredo: Steward
Tarso: Shepherd
Melisa: Shepherdess
Doristo: Mayor
Lariso: Shepherd
Denio: Shepherd
Doña Serafina
Mireno
Lauro: Father of Mireno
A Crier
A Painter

Act I

[Avero and the surrounding areas.]

(The Duke of Avero, an old man, and Don Duarte, the Count of Estremoz, in hunting costume.)

DUKE: Count Duarte, why, just as we're celebrating your arrival in my lands with a hunt, have you in a rage dragged me away to this thicket? Still, as my men are off chasing a boar, speak your mind.

COUNT (raising his sword): Enough dissembling: Draw your long rusty sword and soon enough this naked blade will give you the answer you desire. The sword sometimes serves as the tongue of the wronged, not the pen which mutely cries out your shame.

DUKE: Indeed, the tongue is shaped like the sword, and it prods you to speak ill of me. Now let us curb the tongues in our mouths and let speak the ones in our hands (grasping his sword). But first I'll give you an opportunity to tell me your grievance—not a long one, though, for behavior like yours brooks little patience, for, as I am a gentleman, I've done you no offense.

COUNT: You do a good job of cloaking the crimes that have come to light.

DUKE: Crimes?

COUNT: Does even a man as old as you resort to subterfuge? Duke, keep in mind that no deception of yours can throw me off the track. The answer you ask for is on this paper—with your seal, your handwriting, and your signature. (He throws the paper at him.) Take it, after all, it's yours. The servant you bribed to murder me was shielded by an honest nature as strong as a bronze wall, so strong your money could not pierce it. Here in black and white you commanded him to take my life on my own lands. So much for your feigned surprise when I say you sought my death with a pen and not a sword.

DUKE: I ordered you murdered?
COUNT: This seal, it's yours, isn't it?
DUKE: Yes.
COUNT: And this signature—you can't deny my accusation.
DUKE: Am I awake? Have I gone mad?
COUNT: Read this paper. You will see how just is my vengeful impulse.
DUKE: Good Lord! What sort of tangle is this?

(He reads the letter.)

"To satisfy insults which can only be righted with the death of the Count of Estremoz, I must depend on his trusted servant to carry it out. Accomplish it and come to my estate, where you will be safe and generously rewarded for the danger you endure on my behalf. This note guarantees your safety; return it to the messenger. March 12, 1400. Signed, The Duke."

COUNT: What injury could the house of Estremoz, of which I am Count, have ever done to cause you to stray so from the valor appropriate to one of your ancient blood?
DUKE: These forgeries of my signature and seal must be the work of a traitor harboring an angry secret. His plan is obvious—forge my seal and signature, you die, and then I live in perpetual disgrace. Heaven knows who is guilty and I am innocent, who never in act, speech, or writing sought you harm. If you want a test of this, I'll submit myself to your judgment, and with your help I'll expose the cowardly author of this act this very afternoon. Despite your good reasons for these suspicions, I ask you to contain your just fury and calm your angry breast until you are satisfied. (He sheathes his sword.)
COUNT: Convinced somewhat, I am satisfied.
DUKE (aside): *I have a notion who the author of this insult may be, this figure hiding under my name and seal, and before today's hunt ends he will be unmasked.*
(Enter Figueredo.)
FIGUEREDO (aside): *Oh, how false a secretary can be!*
DUKE: What is this? What accounts for this hurry?
FIGUEREDO: Thank God I found you!
DUKE: Figueredo, what is all this commotion about?

The Timid Young Man at the Palace Gate

FIGUEREDO: We've uncovered a plot woven by your traitorous secretary. He planned to kill the Count of Estremoz this very evening.

COUNT: A plot against me?

FIGUEREDO: Count, you owe your life to me.

COUNT (aside): *Now it's all clear: My seduction and abandonment of Ruy Lorenzo's sister Leonela have come to light.*

DUKE: Thank God justice rushes to the aid of the innocent. And how was this perfidious malice discovered?

FIGUEREDO: In secret he contacted a young man stronger in body than in principles, tapping his greed with the promise to enrich him if he killed the Count; to reassure the youth, he claimed that you were behind this scheme. He agreed to carry out the killing that very night. But this young fellow loved a woman, and, as they say, he who loves is a wastrel of his property and secrets. The bed is a chamber where a woman tortures, not with a lash, but with her mouth and with her touch, and makes even the most discreet man confess. Though charged to be silent about his plan, she was in labor with his secret: She conceived it in her ear, delivered through the mouth, and by midday the birth was announced, and everyone under Avero's bright sun knew of this treachery. When the law took the chatty prisoner away, he confessed that Ruy Lorenzo, who by then had fled with a servant, was his accomplice in this perfidious crime. This is the news I've come to relate.

DUKE: Do you see how heaven has cleared up this whole affair and justified me? Ruy Lorenzo forged my signature. Count, a prudent and wise man would have discovered the truth before lashing out.

COUNT: I do not know what to say, except that only a skilled master in deception could have tricked me into such rashness, and I now deeply regret being fooled by a false pen.

DUKE: From now on I'll be very careful in my choice of a secretary.

COUNT: Since trust is so important, I'll arrange to find one more loyal than clever.

DUKE: It's a miracle you came out of this alive.

COUNT: This treachery has occasioned two results: Disloyalty is fled and the pure light of truth remains secure. By God, how lucky I've been.

DUKE: For such a traitor, no punishment is too great.

COUNT: Humbly, I ask you to forgive me.

DUKE: His guile could have deceived anyone. You are forgiven, Count.

COUNT (aside): *This comes from Leonela's feminine spite; the Duke must remain in the dark about this.*

DUKE: It troubles me that the author of this outrage has got away. But let's be off to find him, and the one who catches or kills him will be awarded all his lands. This whole kingdom will witness a model punishment.

COUNT (to Figueredo): My friend, my life is in your debt, one which will not go unpaid.

(Exeunt omnes. Enter Tarso, a shepherd, and Melisa, a shepherdess.)

MELISA: So, traitor, are you really leaving me?

TARSO: Melisa, you'd better go break in some other colt, this one's tired of you riding him. I've been away from you half a year now, and these six months have cured me of love's sickness. Putting my jealous pangs on a diet, I got better little by little. Now, Melisa, I've come to my senses, and stopped versifying night and day for you! Well, hell's fire to my verses and to me and to you, too. Climbing up Parnassus on a broken-down Muse, I got all battered and bruised. How many names I gave to you—Moon, Stars, Venus…! What quality of yours did I not praise in my verse? Your sighing, your coughing, your silence, your answers, your sitting down, your walking, the color of your skin, your mad disdain of me, even your spitting and sniffling. About all these things I composed sonnets for you. Now, by God, I've slipped out of the net you threw over me, and I don't give a fig for you or your love.

MELISA: Oh Tarso, Tarso, you are indeed a man!—quick to forget. How could this time away cause you to lose your respect for me?

TARSO: You're just a Judas, fickle to the core, even the ever-changing color in your cheeks betrays it.

MELISA: Then give me back the tokens of my love—my ribbons and my locks of hair.

TARSO: What do you think I did with them—decorate my chest or my pack? What a fool! How blind I would have to be to sport the symbols of the harm you did to me. It's been six months, Melisa, since I tossed all that stuff into a fire, those cruel snares of my hopes—locks of hair, silk ribbons, roses, billets-doux, trinkets, assorted bagatelles—all consumed by the flames, never again to bewitch me. Even my pack got tossed into the fire along with all the souvenirs of my madness. To spite your neighbor, sometimes you must burn down your own house.

MELISA: That I must endure this!

TARSO: Go ahead and cry a flood, I still won't trust a woman with Judas-red hair. I know you and your tricky ways. You won't deceive me, by God, even if you weep marrow and urine.

MELISA: Traitor!

TARSO: Here comes the big act! Dry up your two wells, their water is fouled!

MELISA: Cruel beast! I'll be revenged on you!

TARSO: Just how will you do that?

MELISA: By getting married, ungrateful swine.

TARSO: That's taking a shoe and hitting yourself with it.

MELISA: Get out!

TARSO: With pleasure.

MELISA: You're going just like that?

TARSO: By walking away, see?

MELISA: Wait. I bet I know the source of this change of heart.

TARSO: Oh, do you?

MELISA: You're jealous of Mireno.

TARSO: Me jealous of Mireno—the man I serve, whose bread I eat, Lauro's son? His father brought him here as a little boy, and some whisper that though he may dress and work as a shepherd, his outward coarse woolen cloth covers up a nobility that gives honor to our country Portugal.

He's a fine and clever chap, so I grant him your love. But with the free and easy life he leads, I don't think there's a woman around here who can make him start sighing for her.

There's not a shepherd in all of Miño who doesn't like and respect him or maiden who doesn't fancy him. But just look at him, see how handsome he is. If fate had made him cruel and disdainful, there'd be two thousand Echoes pleading for his love and he'd be deaf as Narcissus to all of them. Scorned, you'll come knocking at my door; don't bother, the door to my heart is shut tight.

MELISA: So, it's final; you don't love me.

TARSO: No.

MELISA: Then (making a cross with her fingers) I swear by this cross I'll punish you for this ingratitude.

TARSO: You, punish me?

MELISA: Yes, me. Soon, my false friend, you'll see what troubles I can cause. And when a woman turns her back on a shepherd, he loves her more than ever.

TARSO: Fine!

MELISA: Deceitful one, you'll see what will happen: A shepherd will make you jealous, for when love is lost, jealousy fetches him home. (Exit.)

TARSO: Go now. Despite my brave words, I'm beginning to fear some nasty trick—to ignore the threats of a woman is to turn your back on the devil's pitchfork.

(Enter Mireno, dressed as a shepherd.)

MIRENO: Is that you, Tarso?

TARSO: Mireno, it is indeed, loyal friend, if one who serves you may call himself that.

MIRENO: I've searched for you all day.

TARSO: Melisa kept me here an hour: The more she wept over me, the more I laughed myself to death. But what news is there?

MIRENO: My deep friendship demands I break a plan to you about something, which otherwise I would carry out alone.

TARSO: That you would speak to me in this way comes as a surprise. Since childhood your father Lauro brought me up with you, and now, though I am old enough to be master of my own home, I remain a servant in yours for the love I bear you.

MIRENO: This I well know from long experience. And, along with your love, I've found a sharp mind, exceptional in one of your humble station. So I wish to take you along with me as I seek to discover if my fortune reaches as far as the arrow of my hopes. Long have lofty ambitions, fostered by my proud imagination, whose origin I cannot guess, saddened me. Sometimes I berate unjust heaven for making me a shepherd and not a nobleman. My low station provokes in me a powerful shame and even fear. My thoughts dwell so on this theme that they bring offense to my aged father Lauro. I wonder whether I am truly his son or was I stolen from gentry, but the depth of his love tells me I must be mistaken. A thousand times I've asked him if—as so often is the case—the world on its powerful waves once had lifted him up to its highest, most glorious crest only to cast him down to the sea's floor to drown. Now perhaps he awaits my daring to raise him up again. His refinement, and the fact that he came a newcomer to this land, only encourage the notion that his humble state and rustic look are a disguise of sorts. Even his speech, however much he tries to make it sound native to this place, seems better suited to the court than to these mountains. Tarso, he has always discouraged these fancies of mine, recounting at length tales of a thousand events which run counter to my hopes, insisting that my ancestors were only peasants. Everything he said to humble me only upsets me violently and has driven me to flee this ill-bred life. Now I go in search of the fate the stars have destined for me—for they incline me to great things and promise me many blessings. Besides, if it is a fact that I was born as lowly as I was raised, then the more I make of myself, the more it is to my credit. If you wish to share in my misfortunes or my blessings, this is your chance. Decide now, but do not try to make me change my mind.

TARSO: It's persuasion enough to see you like this. Against such passion I won't counsel or entreat. You are after all a clever fellow, one who studied with the priest. I wish to follow you, but I can't help thinking of Lauro and this new worry for him.

MIRENO: If my fortune thrives, I hope to God that I can change his grief to joy.

TARSO: When are you off?

MIRENO: Right away.

TARSO: Today?

MIRENO: This moment.

TARSO: And with what money?

MIRENO: I have enough here from the two oxen I sold. Let's go straight to Avero, where I'll buy you a sword and hat.

TARSO: Please God we don't come back like old dogs, battered and beaten! (Exeunt Tarso and Mireno.)

[Another part of the forest.]

(Enter Ruy Lorenzo and Vasco, lackey.)

VASCO: Sir, go back into the forest; we'll only be here an hour before they catch up with us. The peasants in the farmhouses around here must be searching for us like greyhounds after a hare, and if they catch us there'll be a second Crucifixion, but this time, for our sins, instead of a remembrance there'll be a dismembrance!

RUY: Vasco, survival is no longer in the cards; even if heaven shields us from all our pursuers, vile hunger, with its lowly weapons that sap the strength of even the most stolid, will hand us over to the Duke.

VASCO: It's true that there is no sword to smite all-powerful hunger.

RUY: Besides, I am an ill-starred wretch forever estranged from success. I even failed to avenge my sister's honor, stolen by the Count of Estremoz, first with a scheme involving forging his signature, then arranging an assassination; so let my life be ended now. While I hold a sword, I will not perish from hunger.

VASCO: Can it be that someone who thinks himself a man through and through could have gone to all the trouble you have to discover whether or not your sister had been raped? Really, do you believe that any woman in the whole world has ever been raped?

RUY: How can you doubt it? Beyond my reckoning, books, tales, and paintings depict violent rapes and attacks of women.

VASCO: I'd laugh at what you say if I didn't reckon we are to dine at the Lord's table this night, though, to tell the truth, I'd settle for a snack in this world and then go to bed in the dark.

Take a step back and listen: If Leonela hadn't wanted the grapes in her vineyard plucked, she had but to follow the example of the hedgehog: hunch herself up, then scratch, bite, and make a fool of her abuser, thus leaving her reputation intact and her melon with no bite taken out of it. In the middle of a field, a mare will defend herself among a herd of nags, and she can't moan, "Oh heavens, they're taking my honor from me!" as a virtuous woman can at such a critical moment. To escape an agile tom and other alley cats, a tiny female cat will have the pluck to jump over roofs and attics, and she's only able to hiss and say, "Meow." And are these tarts trying to persuade us that they can't protect their belongings from the perils of the night? I promise you that if the law put the raped along with the rapists behind the oars of a galley, there'd be fewer women attacked and they would be more virtuous.

(Enter Tarso and Mireno.)

TARSO: Melisa swore revenge against me. It'll be sweet when she sees that I've given her the slip.

MIRENO: How badly you repay her love.

TARSO: Damn the woman! She's as changeable as a band of gypsies. She can keep her loving words, all her tones sweeter than an organ's notes. All I want is to follow you over land and sea, and to give up love for war.

RUY: I hear people.

VASCO: You're right—and I'm so scared I can't spit.

RUY: We're finished.

VASCO: Heaven help us. If there exists some patron saint of lackeys, get me out of this jam!

RUY: Calm down, they're only a couple of peasants without any weapons to fight or defend themselves. They're not going to do us much harm.

VASCO: I hope to God that's so!

RUY: Besides, their relaxed manner should quiet our fears.

VASCO: Saint Anthony, blind them!

RUY: Quiet, we're upon them. Good friends, where are you on your way to?

MIRENO: Gentlemen, we're off to town to buy some things. Is the Duke there?

RUY: Yes.

MIRENO: May heaven preserve him. And you, where are you off to? This path breaks from the Royal Road and leads to some farmhouses at the foot of these mountains.

RUY: Your words bespeak kindness, shepherd friend, and so I feel obliged to explain my lot. To avenge the shaming of a sister, I tried to slay a powerful man. Uncovering my honorable daring, the Duke sent his men into the forest to track me down and take me prisoner. Desperate to save myself, I've come to the roadway. Now, when honor is pursued by so many, I say, take my life.

MIRENO: Your words soften my heart, and, by God, though miserly fortune made me a poor shepherd, I swear I was also endowed with rich blood, and so I take your side. To save you we must exchange our costumes: Don these humble ones for yours, and in this disguise preserve yourself until that time when heaven begins to smile on you. A good strategy can overcome many troubles.

RUY: Oh what a noble heart beats beneath a coarse coat! You show such valor as before I've never seen. May heaven repay this kindness, for surely I cannot.

MIRENO: We must be quick. Let's go into the woods and exchange our clothing.

RUY: Let us be off. How blessed I have been! (Exeunt Ruy and Mireno.)

TARSO: And are you going to swap my coat for this quilt-like thing of yours that looks like so much beef stew?

VASCO: Yes, though it grieves me.

TARSO: Then you'll have to give me a couple of lessons first, so my hand can find my way around the entrances and exits of this Troy, for even our village priest, who knows a thing or two and can even sing hymns for the dead, couldn't dress me for the role of King David in the Corpus Christi play. Just as we have schoolmasters to teach schoolboys to read, we should have teachers to show us how to put on breeches.

VASCO: Let's be off; you'll soon catch on.

(Exeunt Vasco and Tarso. Enter the Mayor Doristo, and Lariso and Denio, shepherds.)

DORISTO: Now I know just what they look like and how they're dressed, master and man. Be quiet now or you'll wish you had been.

LARISO: On what account would he want to kill the Count—the scoundrel!

DORISTO: By heaven, if the devil doesn't hide 'em, I'll catch this pair and bring 'em back to Avero in shackles and stocks.

DENIO: What sort of beast can carry 'em if they're in stocks?

DORISTO: Keep to your own affairs, Constable. Do I clutch this staff of office for nothing? Am I not the Mayor? I say your donkey will carry them in stocks 'til we reach the town of Avero.

The Timid Young Man at the Palace Gate

LARISO: Let's look for 'em, and afterwards we'll figure out about how they'll go.

DORISTO: The whole mountain's surrounded; they can't get away on foot.

DENIO: Both of 'em, servant and master, got to be here hidden someplace.

LARISO: Everythin's in my noggin: I got their descriptions of their clothes—hat, cloak, doublets.

DORISTO: If we catch 'em, for payment I'll ask the Duke to put up a gallows next to the elm…

LARISO: If you can get a gallows put up, you're one sharp fellow.

DORISTO: …so fine that it'll be an honor to hear someone tell you, "Get hanged." (Exeunt omnes.)

(Enter Ruy dressed as a shepherd, and Mireno as a gentleman.)

RUY: Courtly apparel sits so well on you that I would take you for one of high rank had I not first seen you with your handsome shape hidden beneath this coarse suit of clothes.

Often when a peasant dons the trappings of a noble, he bears the posture of an oak. He can't move hands or feet, looking nothing so much as a mud wall covered with a silk rug. But when I see the grace with which you move and command these clothes, you give an air of dignity, like gold covered by a coarse cloak. From this I sense some nobility in you, and I feel the same esteem for you as for the Duke of Avero. May heaven make you as good a man as he is.

MIRENO: And may you return undisguised and serene in peace, and overcome through patience the outrages of fortune. Should my father see you in this costume, you will find in him a new refuge. Trust in him, and tell him that my fancy for the life of the soldier takes me from him, but I hope to God that someday I'll be able to provide him with a happy old age.

RUY: Farewell, gallant youth. I keep this sword only to ward off harm from those who might recognize me.

MIRENO: You do the right thing. Go, and go with God's blessings. Though we're off to town, we needn't worry, for once we're there we'll buy swords.

(Enter Vasco dressed as a shepherd.)

VASCO: Let's be out of here, there's no point in tarrying. I wish we were a hundred leagues away already.

MIRENO: And what can Tarso be doing?

VASCO: Over there disentangling his breeches, and maybe even buttoning them up. He's got a wind up 'cause I pinched his sword, but without it I'm not worth a thing.

MIRENO: Delay is dangerous.

RUY: My friend, good-bye.

VASCO: You cut a fine picture in the doublet.

RUY: Never will I forget this act of kindness.

VASCO: You know, that coat doesn't look bad on you. But how about me: A lackey has been crammed into a shepherd. (Exeunt Vasco and Ruy.)

MIRENO: The idle horse, his appetite and hunger satisfied by fields of green grass, saunters leisurely and unconcerned, his bit dangling from his harness. But when, for some festivity, he is adorned with gay trappings and harnesses and enameled gold, the beast seems to exhale silver-colored foam, his hooves start tearing at the ground, the bells adorning, his cinch shaking. In the same way, though I grew up among the oak and the evergreen, hearing a rustic tongue and wearing coarse cloth, this courtly costume awakens my noble aspirations, for fine clothing makes pride grow.

(Enter Tarso dressed in the breeches of Vasco.)

TARSO: Do you see these spools of thread I'm forced to wear? I'll never find my way in this fancy and complicated confusion of streets and intersections. Did you ever see so many slices—these breeches have enough of them to be a melon! Will you tell me what astrologer has an astrolabe less intelligible: I've been at this an hour and still haven't stumbled on the pocket. So help me, what sort of an inventor could have come up with such a tangled construction? What genius!

MIRENO: Enough, Tarso.

TARSO: Don't be surprised if this hasn't been the work of a mere man.

MIRENO: Then of what?

TARSO: Of an enchanter, worthy of Merlin, because in these astrolabes the greatest sages will not find a beginning or an end. But now that I've been impressed into the lackey's army and you've been made a gentleman, what shall we do?

MIRENO: Go to Avero, for this costume has raised my hopes; I'm off to try new adventures.

TARSO: You seek to fly to the heavens, but I fear we'll end up in the mud. But now that you've become another man, a gentleman, perhaps you should change your name, since Mireno is no name for a gentleman.

MIRENO: Yes, you're right. I'm no shepherd now, and must rid myself of the name of Mireno. "Don Dionís" is an illustrious and renowned name in Portugal—from today on, call me Don Dionís.

TARSO: Not a bad choice, since with this name the kings of this country won great praise. Now that you've risen up in the world, give me a suitable name for a lackey in these breeches, for I've given up the name of Tarso.

MIRENO: Choose one yourself.

TARSO: I'll choose—if it's all right with you. What do you think of...?

MIRENO: What?

TARSO: Gómez Brito. What do you think?

MIRENO: Perfect.

TARSO: Well, that's sharp thinking, by God! Though we may not be bishops, we've just confirmed ourselves.

(Enter Doristo, Lariso, Denio,
and shepherds with sticks and ropes.)

DORISTO: Damnation! How we gonna find 'em?

LARISO: Unless they know how to fly, they gotta be somewhere in these shrubs and boulders.

DENIO: Let's look for 'em in the open. Isn't that them?

DORISTO: Keep your voice down.

LARISO: By God, they fit their descriptions.

DORISTO: Tie up their arms; you can see they don't have weapons.

DENIO: Surrender, young fellow.

LARISO: In the name of the King, halt.

DORISTO: In the name of the Mayor, halt.

(They seize them from behind, tying them up.)

MIRENO: What is this?

TARSO: Are you all mad? Why are you taking us prisoners?

DORISTO: For being the thieves you are! (to his companions) Oh, how these tricksters talk! (to Mireno and Tarso) You know you're them what plotted to kill the Count, and now you ask us why we've taken you prisoner.

DENIO: That's a good one!

TARSO: Count? What Count? What murder? Have you ever seen us before?

DORISTO: The hangman will let you know all about it when he strings you up by the gills and the Adam's apple.

MIRENO: If I were carrying my sword, you'd regret this!

TARSO: The clothing swap put us in this mess. My good sir, Don Dionís, are these the spoils of war? What sort of deception did you fall into? What a mistake you made.

DORISTO: What sort of gibberish is this?

TARSO: I want to be Tarso, not Brito, a shepherd, not a lackey. I want my coat instead of these breeches. Oh, I cry for the pleasures of my youth.

LARISO: Listen, scoundrel, keep your trap shut—unless you'd like a slug in the snout.

DORISTO: It's to Avero we're off.

MIRENO: Have courage. Once in Avero, and the Duke has seen us, all this will be cleared up before any harm comes to us.

DORISTO: At last, our town will get a gallows!

DENIO: Yes, and if we put it up under the elm, we can hold our meetings there.

TARSO: I got no complaints about anything except these damned breeches. Whoever had to endure such a trial?

MIRENO: What are you going on about? What's troubling you?

TARSO: If I end up swinging, like Judas—and even he was never a lackey—don't I have a right to weep and wail? Today they're going to stretch my neck.

DORISTO: I'm going to put a clock in the scaffold's gibbet. Let's be on our way.

LARISO: You'll bring glory to our hamlet.

TARSO: If you're looking to escape somewhere, hide in these breeches of mine! (Exeunt all.)

[A room in the Duke's palace.]

(Enter Doña Juana and Don Antonio in travelling clothes.)

JUANA: Cousin, Don Antonio!

ANTONIO: Hush: Don't call me by name. Don't make a fuss over me. The Duke must not discover that I'm in Avero. I am on my way to Galicia, summoned by my King, Don Juan, who has ever been kind and caring to me. Making a detour in my journey, I've come here to learn whether all that is said about the beauty of the Duke's two daughters is true or just a fabrication of the flighty masses.

JUANA: To be sure, there is a good deal here worth seeing and admiring. But will yours be a brief stay, denying me the joy of your company?

ANTONIO: If the Duke should recognize me and compel me to stay, this would be an affront to the King.

JUANA: Then we'll do as you wish. But if the Duke discovers that Don Antonio de Barcelo, the Count of Penela, has stayed in his home without his knowledge, he would sorely regret having missed the chance to serve you. No gentleman has ever visited him, who, through the firm laws of hospitality, did not find lodging.

ANTONIO: Of course he would; after all, he is the grandson of Portugal's king. But, Cousin, putting that aside, tell me this: Is the exalted beauty of his daughters truly so great as is claimed?

JUANA: Is this just curiosity? Or perhaps your heart has been wounded by blind Cupid's arrow?

ANTONIO: His jabs are not likely to make me moan before I've even caught sight of them. No, it's just youthful curiosity that brings me to Avero. How could I love what I've not yet seen?

JUANA: That you could say such a thing is hurtful, for our nation has a boast above all others: Love has a home here, and is welcomed by all Portuguese. Love captures the Spaniard through the eye, the Portuguese through the ear. And the Duke's daughters are worthy of our nation's fame. The older one, whom the Duke of Berganza plans to give to his son and heir, the Count of Vasconcelos, possesses such beauty that if Zeus were but to glance at her it would send Hera into a

jealous rage. And then there is the other sister, Doña Serafina. Her beauty is divine.
ANTONIO: And, Cousin, which of the two do you judge the more beautiful?
JUANA: My taste is more inclined to the older one, although the common prattle takes the side of the younger. But, of course, in matters of taste there can be no debate, and even more so when it comes to the heart. Avero is divided into two camps on this issue. Either can be praised as the more beautiful.
ANTONIO: Have any nobles shown a serious interest in them?
JUANA: Yes, Don Francisco and Don Duarte.
ANTONIO: How close to making a claim are they?
JUANA: More than one nosey body says that each wants to marry one of the daughters.
ANTONIO: Cousin, I will see the sisters this afternoon, and, after that, I must be off.
JUANA: I'll place you where their beauty may just cause you a pang or two.
ANTONIO: Which? Serafina or Madalena?
JUANA: I can't say; both are beauties. But the Duke's coming with them now. Stand over here.

[Doña Juana and Don Antonio stand apart, concealed from the others.]

(Enter the Duke, Count Don Duarte, Serafina, and Madalena.)

DUKE: Count, let everything proceed this way.
COUNT: As you know, the King, our master, favors the house of Berganza's heir and requests that you give your elder daughter to him as his wife. Will you then write His Majesty saying that Serafina, with his pleasure and permission, will be mine?
DUKE: Agreed.
COUNT: I believe the King looks upon me with affection, and will think this a fine thing. I will write him, also.
DUKE: Though Portuguese, she is not possessed of a passionate nature, and not inclined to surrender her freedom to a man. So, until we hear that the King decides that she should give her hand to you, don't let on about this to Serafina.

The Timid Young Man at the Palace Gate

JUANA: These girls caught your eye soon enough. Tell me, Don Antonio, what do you think of these sisters.

ANTONIO: I can't decide to which my soul is more inclined, or what it's commanding me to do. Madalena is beautiful, but Serafina is the sun of Portugal. When I look at her my soul swallows the flames of love from her snowy white flesh. The fame of her beauty runs short of the mark.

DUKE: This is an important matter.

ANTONIO: In her beauty she is a Phoenix.

DUKE: Madalena, please join the Count and me.

COUNT (to Serafina): *Since the Duke has given us the opportunity, Serafina, I wish to speak to you—if I dare fly so high that I reach the Seraphim.*

ANTONIO: Cousin, my soul flees through my eyes, gradually losing passion's battle, which, in losing, I win.

JUANA: Cousin, you came here sane, but I think you will leave mad.

DUKE: My daughter, the King offers you his respect and honor. Mark what a blessing this is for you.

MADALENA: My will is a wax for Your Grace to imprint on it the stamp that he finds most suitable. For me there is but silence and obedience.

DUKE: A thousand times blessed is the father who hears such a thing.

COUNT (to Serafina): *My joys having climbed to their summit will, I fear, come falling down.*

SERAFINA (to the Count): *Count, your musings I neither understand nor find pleasing.*

COUNT (to Serafina): *A seraph can easily grasp the end and the essence of an argument. Serafina, you must not pretend you don't understand what to you must be plain as day.*

SERAFINA (to the Count): *My lord, you do talk a great deal.*

COUNT (to Serafina): *What can you expect, since I am but a mortal? God ordains that men explain their intentions with words. Were we like you, a seraph, we would speak to one another with just our thoughts.*

SERAFINA (to the Count): *Does love go on so?*

COUNT (to Serafina): *It must speak, mustn't it?*

SERAFINA (to the Count): *No. One shouldn't trust Cupid, and a babbler even less.*

COUNT (to Serafina): *Heaven, with a generous hand, has made you perfect in every way.*

ANTONIO: Cousin, you would not expect such cleverness from one so lovely. How sharply she answers! Now the heavens have glazed over love with jealousy. I find this Count a disagreeable fellow.

JUANA: Pity your hopes if such an adversary assails them.

DUKE: I need a secretary in whom I can place my confidence. Many have sought this post, depending on favor to assist them, but few understood what it entails. It will cost me much effort to be without one at such a time.

MADALENA: If only he'd been loyal, the last one would have been ideal.

DUKE: Yes, indeed he was, but he put my life and reputation at risk.

(Enter shepherds, bringing Mireno and Tarso as prisoners.)

DORISTO: Quicken the step of the scoundrel.

LARISO: Here's the Duke.

TARSO: May Herod give me patience.

DENIO: Get up there; you're the mayor, talk to him.

DORISTO: Oh, my fine old fellow, I'm the Mayor and you're the Duke...

LARISO (To the Duke): You shall see... (to Doristo). Fine so far, but get closer to him.

DORISTO: We found out, I mean me and the blacksmith and his wife, we heard you'd ordered these good-for-nothins taken prisoner, and us, Bras Llorente and Gil Bragado, went.... After calling a council, the constable Pero Mínguez.... (to Lariso) Get over here, you're not a horse, tell the rest.

LARISO: I don't want to tell it, you do it.

DORISTO: I only got the story in my mind up to now; but in contusion, these be the crooks we caught just for your pleasure, me and Gil Mingullo. Do as the people wills, Your Dukiness, and don't forget what I said about the scaffold.

DUKE: What simplemindedness. I can't figure out what you've come about, or why you're holding these men. Loose the prisoners; you two tell me what grievances you've committed that you should be brought here in this fashion.

MIRENO (on his knees): Great sir, my only crime was to grant assistance to an unfortunate man, hounded and harassed by your people and power. If exchanging clothes with him to save his life is rash offense in your eyes, then I am guilty.

DUKE: You freed my secretary? But, of course … these clothes were his. Tell me, traitor, why did you grant him this kindness?

MIRENO: Your Grace, don't insult me or attach that name to me, for I am unaccustomed to such scorn.

DUKE: Just who are you?

MIRENO: I am no one. But I will be, for in order to be more than I am, I put aside what I was for the sake of what I shall be.

DUKE: What is it you're saying?

MADALENA (aside): *This is rare boldness. His fearlessness bespeaks deep-seated courage. His misfortune troubles me.*

DUKE: Tell me, did you know the traitor you gave help to? But surely you knew who he was, why else would you have put yourself in such peril?

MIRENO: I knew that he wished to slay one who dishonored his sister and that he later informed you of his honorable aim. When your men sought to take him prisoner, I saved him from you. And, truth to tell, I was shocked to see you pursue the aggrieved and showing favor to the true offender.

COUNT (aside): *What is this? Is the news of the shame I brought to Leonela being spread about?*

DUKE: Do you know who it was who dishonored her?

MIRENO: If I only knew that, my lord…

DUKE: It was the cunning of the traitor who deceived you. You know where he is, you must—if you seek your freedom, tell us.

MIRENO: What a fine thing to commit such villainy out of fear, even if I knew his whereabouts.

DUKE: Villainy to expose a traitor? Take him prisoner. Unless this man has lost his senses and disdains living, he'll tell us where he's hidden.

MADALENA (aside): *I seek to set him free this very moment, for no one of such merit deserves such treatment.*

DUKE: Count, I seek to avenge you.

COUNT: He will not stay silent.

TARSO (aside): *For sure, some great joy will come of this for me.*

DUKE: Let us be off, I wish to give the King his answer.
TARSO (aside): *Hasn't this change of name and state turned out well for us!*
DUKE: Tell me where he is and your life will be spared.
MIRENO (aside): *I must have heart, for Fortune has come to my aid. It is her nature to start off badly and to end up well.*
TARSO (aside): *Breeches, if ever we're separated, nevermore will we be reunited.*

[Tarso and Mireno are taken off as prisoners.]

DUKE: Make a request of someone in my chambers and you'll receive the payment you deserve.
DORISTO: You're a sharp fellow, tell 'em what we want.
LARISO: Well...
DORISTO: For the trouble we've gone to, sir, could you make a gallows in my village? A real fine one, so we could hang even the most respectable man on it? (Exit the shepherds, the Duke, and the Count.)
MADALENA: It grieves me, Serafina, to see that man prisoner.
SERAFINA: I allow that his fine manner inclines me to intercede for him.
MADALENA: Is this the way your feelings lean? Are you already taken with his manner? Well, even if you wanted to, you won't be able to free him.
SERAFINA: I hope you're wrong. (Exeunt Madalena and Serafina.)
JUANA: Must you go away this afternoon?
ANTONIO: Oh, Cousin, how can I if I've lost my way, if I'm blind, if that valiant coward, cowardly valiant love has won the whole treasure of my heart and my will. I won't leave until tomorrow.
JUANA: You're doing just fine! Finally, you're in love.
ANTONIO: I suspect, dear Cousin, that Serafina will be the angel who flies away with my peace and happiness.

ACT II

MADALENA: Oh, what strange feelings, what lofty thoughts are these? What baseless towers have been raised up in the air? Oh, mad fancies, how daringly they speed! For such small delights they seek to expose my weakness to the judgments of gossips and the opinion of the common tongue.

The Timid Young Man at the Palace Gate

My hopes, which yesterday floated on a serene and tranquil sea sheltered by heaven from any harm, now are beset by sleeplessness. I gave my consent to the Count of Vasconcelos—or rather to my father for him—but, taken by surprise, passion stormed my heart with my honor offering no resistance. I may be faulted, for I saw the risk, but, as we all know, love is a child, blind and foolish. To my sorrow I ask my heart: Are you to surrender yourself to a man who is a stranger and a prisoner? Isn't it right to love the Count? But, oh, how desire tramples reason. Now that, at my entreaty, my father has freed him and declared his innocence, my madness will disappear. Since he's a stranger, if he goes away without much trouble, patience will cure my distempered passions. Time and absence are expert physicians when it comes to love.

But what sort of harsh treatment do I employ to cure my illness? If the wound can be healed, it's cruelty to sever the limb. Since the sight of him excites me, I'll give love a little time. Love is a fever of the mind lasting sometimes but a single day, and no one would deny a thirsty sick man a drop of water.

I'll call him here: Doña Juana.... But wait, check your runaway impulses, lest you spin out of control. Do you seek to make public your dishonor? Oh, let your shame overcome your mad hunger: For if it is madness to let love into your heart, it's even madder and more shameful to speak of it.

(Enter Juana.)

JUANA: That dashing fellow, 'til now a prisoner, and through your intervention set free, seeks to speak with you.

MADALENA (aside): *How swiftly love strives to seize a chance and good fortune to carry out its desires. But he is wise, for love is all a matter of opportunity.* Do you know what he wants?

JUANA: He wishes to communicate his gratitude for the kindness he's received at your hands.

MADALENA (aside): *He sells roses enclosing asps.*

JUANA: Shall I let him in?

MADALENA (aside): *If the prisoner can imprison, if the abused can abuse, if the bound can bind my feelings, what will he do now here and free?* Tell him to return in the afternoon; say that I'm busy now.... No, tell him not to come back.

JUANA: I'm going.

MADALENA: Listen, tell him to wait ... but be off, it's late.

JUANA: Should he come back?

MADALENA: Isn't that what I said? Now go.

JUANA: I'll do as you wish.

MADALENA: But come back. I wouldn't want him to feel offended in some way.

JUANA: What shall I tell him?

MADALENA: To leave ... (aside) *and take me with him.* Go tell him to come in...

JUANA: I'll go to him then. (Exit.)

MADALENA: Though he may be right in front of me, today my Portuguese strength will resist and triumph. In both the virtuous woman and the other sort there is a natural longing to see and to possess what pleases. The difference between the two is this: The honorable woman remains silent, the other cries out her need.

I shall be mute: In that way I can disguise my disquiet—if a fire can be covered without smoke betraying its presence. I'll be able to smother it if I consume the time in empty chatter ... though love's tyrannous flames fly out through windows the moment you close the doors on them. If the mouth should contain them, they would escape through the eyes.... I can silence love's mad tongue and my passions won't be seen, but passion comes out in tiny ways, like signs from my eyes—signs too small to embolden a lover to try to plunder love's spoils.

(Enter Mireno dressed as a gentleman.)

MIRENO: Though it is a great boldness for someone of so little worth to come into your presence, my lady, I have come to show my gratitude for the kindness I've received—for there is no worse sin than ingratitude. Because I protected the life of a poor unfortunate—which for a noble is an obligation—I found myself persecuted and imprisoned. But clearly heaven also revealed to me the other side of the coin, since, by your assistance, I am once again free. Did I say "free"? I badly misspoke. For when a nobleman receives a kindness, he lives a slave and a prisoner to his benefactor. Ah, were my life such that I should remain a slave to you, then I could repay some part of this kindness done me. Though

The Timid Young Man at the Palace Gate

I may seem base compared to those lofty gentlemen who come to you surrendering themselves (he kneels), I offer my life to you, for I can give you no more.

MADALENA: Rise from the floor.

MIRENO: My lady, this is where I belong.

MADALENA: Do as I tell you. (aside) *Who is this who blinds my heart? Heaven help me!* Are you Portuguese?

MIRENO (he rises): I imagine so.

MADALENA: What do you mean, "imagine"? Are you saying you're uncertain who you are?

MIRENO: When I was very young my father brought me to the place where he now dwells and where he owns some property. He's considered a worthy fellow, and I think we come from Portugal.

MADALENA: Are you a nobleman?

MIRENO: I believe so. My natural instincts seem to indicate that I'm more than I seem to be.

MADALENA: If called upon, would your actions demonstrate their nobility?

MIRENO: I believe so. I've never failed to perform as a noble should.

MADALENA: Before each statement you say, "I believe." Perhaps you think I'm asking you to recite the "Apostles Creed."

MIRENO: For the favor you've granted me, my lady is free to ask me to recite it, if that is her pleasure.

MADALENA: You certainly are grateful. What is your name?

MIRENO: Don Dionís.

MADALENA: Then I take you for a Portuguese and a man of illustrious heritage, for no common man in this kingdom bears such a name, a royal surname. It's only because I imagined that you were a man of honor that I was moved to intervene with my father to free you.

MIRENO: My life is your debt.

MADALENA: So, then, now that you're free, what do you plan to do once you leave here? Where are you thinking of going?

MIRENO: My lady, I intend to go wherever my fame can rise above my lofty thoughts; this alone drives me from my country.

MADALENA: And where will this fortune be found?

MIRENO: In war—there my courage will enable me to gain the fame I seek.

MADALENA: Couldn't you reach this goal following a peaceful path?

MIRENO: In what way?

MADALENA: Easily, if you devise a plan to fill the vacant post of secretary to my father.

MIRENO: I wasn't born with the inclination to serve, but for something higher.

MADALENA: Know that a plumed feather will help you soar when you decide to fly.

MIRENO: How can I fly with just one feather?

MADALENA: On the wings of patronage; at court the flight of favor can soar above a thousand obstacles.

MIRENO: As we often see among men in high places, dependence on favor leads to fear, an unworthy impulse.

MADALENA: Don Dionís, this is my desire.

MIRENO: If it is Your Grace's desire that I serve the Duke, it will be done. My lady, I feel of a sudden that I've been lofted to the highest of all points, the "primum mobile." If I bring you pleasure, I cannot rise higher. If the Duke accepts me, I shall be his secretary.

MADALENA: I've done all this to see you prosper. Having given you your freedom, it would grieve me to see you throw it away in war. So stay here, and I'll see to it that you get this post.

MIRENO: For such munificence may heaven keep you for a thousand years.

MADALENA (aside): *Honor, flee, for perfidious love is about to escape my mouth.* (Exit.)

MIRENO: What should I make of all this? What can I conclude from all that I have seen? Now that my fancies have soared to the clouds, let my thoughts unbosom themselves and tell me if so much kindness can stem from nothing more than her worthy nature. Or am I wrong to think that love has come to play a role here?

Lord, what a mad idea! Let not my mind be so daring and bold as to even consider such a thing. My humility must smother the winds which raise up my inconstant wishes. What reckless presumption driven by my hopes leads me to imagine that the woman who makes me a secretary loves me in secret?

But, wait, didn't I gain my freedom because of her? And just now,

The Timid Young Man at the Palace Gate

didn't I see affection quite clearly in her eyes? Yes, she must be in love with me. Stop, I must stop saying such things. It's simply wrong to imagine that kindness, born of her nobility and bestowed as an act of generosity, is at root love.

But her desire to know my name, my country, if I am noble—doesn't that stem from love? No. This is madness. Well, if not love, what else—feminine curiosity? Yes, but if love had not taken rule of her tongue, would she have said, "Don Dionís, this is my desire." This argument is a powerful one, isn't it? Yes, very! But my lowly nature cannot be convinced that it can take flight and rise to the heavens of such beauty … but since when has my breast been the seat of such cowardice? I must wait. Fleeting time will always make certain what is doubtful. Money and love cannot stay hidden long.

(Enter Tarso.)

TARSO: As Daniel was saved from the lions, the daughter of the Duke has got us out of jail—where I stayed with less patience than he did. But why do we want to wait around? Have we had such a good time of it up 'til now?

Was Avero so good to us we should be slow in leaving it? Let's be on our way. But now you're going to tell me this is where you'll become a gentleman. True, by the Duke's command we were nearly made knights, not riding horses but asses, flogged through the streets. It's true too we did get dubbed, even if it was with a whip and not a sword, and on our backs not our shoulders.

MIRENO: Brito, my friend.

TARSO: I'm not Brito, but Tarso.

MIRENO: Listen, fool.

TARSO: Damn these nuisance breeches! Since you're the one who transformed me into Brito, you can free me from these fetters! I didn't seek to travel all over to end up in shackles like a criminal. Get me out of these things!

MIRENO: Tarso, you wonder of nature—will you never be serious? Your talk is all nonsense.

TARSO: I'm reduced to a pair of breeches! But tell me what news you have.

MIRENO: I am nothing less than the secretary to the Duke of Avero.

TARSO: Come again!

MIRENO: She who engineered this generous deed is the same woman who got us freed.

TARSO: I better remove anything you're carrying; you're standing on stilts.

MIRENO: Wait, there's more.

TARSO: Congratulations. The first thing you can do in your new post is get me out of these breeches.

(Exeunt Mireno and Tarso. Enter Don Antonio and Juana.)

ANTONIO: Though the King awaits me, my love compels me to remain here, for now my desire is my only king. Loving from afar would consume me with anguished passion, but nearness to her relieves my pain. Like a curious bird who did not see that the lovely branch he perched on was limed, I am now a prisoner of love, and when I try to fly I only get more stuck.

The worthy Count of Estremoz courts and merits Serafina. I've learned he is favored by the Duke to be his son-in-law, so I shall remain here, for, as they say, "he who doesn't turn up is turned out." Away from here I could not find comfort in absence or forgetfulness. Here, if my beloved Serafina were to take notice of me and reciprocate my love, my happiness would be certain, my hopes sure. Then I could go away happy and confident. I could entrust my life to her pledge—if a wise man can ever trust the sun in January or a woman who is not near at hand.

She does not know me or my torments, so my best hope is to stay here, and besides, whether I see the King now or later really doesn't matter much. So, dear Cousin, if you don't wish to see me weep and the world to learn of a doleful end for me away from her, don't counsel me to leave Avero.

JUANA: Antonio, you know full well that I respect your desires and show you all the love due a blood relative and head of a family. If I try to keep you from staying, it's because this is a small village and your presence would be the subject of talk.

ANTONIO: I can live here without drawing attention to myself. The Duke, because his last secretary committed a crime and lives in exile, seeks a secretary, and, though we've corresponded, he has never seen me.

JUANA: It makes me laugh to think how you've solved your problem.

The Timid Young Man at the Palace Gate

ANTONIO: Living in the palace, concealed in this post, I'll be able to lay the foundation of my hopes, as time, opportunity, and your assistance may make them thrive.

JUANA: The ruse, Cousin, though a clever one, is hardly suitable to someone of your station.

ANTONIO: Love ennobles all stations. As long as I am not away from her, I shall be honored by any post.

JUANA: Then look for a way to do it.

ANTONIO: The most pressing problem has already been taken care of.

JUANA: What?

ANTONIO: I sent a petition for the post to the Duke.

JUANA: How industrious you've been, but I must fault you for not letting me know of it.

ANTONIO: Good luck is the offspring of great care. The steward has taken charge of my request, and I hear that the Duke has confidence in his judgment.

JUANA: He is a trusted favorite of the Duke.

ANTONIO: If that steward keeps his promise, and heaven seeks to gratify my desires, I expect some great joy.

JUANA: Cousin, the Duke is coming.

(Enter the Duke and Figueredo.)

DUKE: You realize now that this post requires a person with several qualities—noble birth, good bearing, discretion, and a fine hand.

FIGUEREDO: Of his rank I cannot speak, but of these other traits I assure Your Grace there is no one in Portugal better qualified to hold this post; as to his hand, Your Grace should be satisfied by the petition you hold.

DUKE: Stop, your praise makes me wish to see him.

FIGUEREDO: I'd go and summon him—but he's already right in front of Your Grace. Come over here, young gentleman, my master, the Duke, wishes to see you.

ANTONIO: I kneel at Your Grace's feet.

DUKE: Rise. Where are you from?

ANTONIO: My birthplace was Lisbon, sir.

DUKE: You have served whom?

ANTONIO: My childhood companion was Duke Antonio of Barcelona, Count of Penela, from whom I bear letters favorable to my aspirations.

DUKE: Though I've never seen him, the valor others credit him with endears him to me. Why did you withhold these missives from me?

ANTONIO: I'm not accustomed to soliciting favors that may be sought in person. Besides, I wanted Your Grace to see me first.

DUKE: Steward, this man's appearance and manner please me. (to Don Antonio) As of now you are my secretary: Let your task be carried out with all the promise of your bearing.

ANTONIO: I'll leave that to a judgment of how I carry out my tasks.

DUKE: Doña Juana, what are Serafina and Madalena doing?

JUANA: Just now the two were in the garden, although I understand my lady Doña Madalena was slightly indisposed.

DUKE: What's wrong with her?

JUANA: For two days she's been gloomy, but it's not clear why.

DUKE: Let's go and see her, but I can guess the source of her despond. My plan for the change in her life, as it would for any honorable woman, has brought this on. She fears, I would guess, being a prisoner for life.
   Doña Juana, stay here; the messenger is on his way from Lisbon, and since he knows your cousin, the Count of Penela, you will have things to ask him.

JUANA: That's true, sir.

DUKE: Secretary, it is my wish you stay behind.

ANTONIO: I kneel at your feet. (Exeunt the Duke and Figueredo.)

ANTONIO: This has begun fortunately.

JUANA: If you think it fortunate to become the servant of an equal, you're very fortunate.

ANTONIO: My presence here is important: It stands between my passion and the jealousy the Count of Estremoz stirs up in me.

JUANA: The woman you adore cares precious little about him and is so oblivious to him that at this very moment her sole concern is rehearsing a verse play with her waiting ladies. Tomorrow is Shrove Tuesday and she plans to present it for her sister, without the Duke's knowledge.

ANTONIO: Is she much taken with poetry?

The Timid Young Man at the Palace Gate

JUANA: She's beside herself over anything poetical; this afternoon, dressed in male costume, she is rehearsing a role with me.

ANTONIO: Is this the way you say such a thing?

JUANA: Well, how would you have me say it?

ANTONIO: By asking of me in recompense for such joy my life, my heart, my mind! For this may your life have more years than there are stars, may cruel time never consume your beauty. For this may your desires all be satisfied and the King of Portugal fall in love with you, give you his hand, his scepter, and his life...

JUANA: Slow down. You've taken leave of your senses. Soon you'll have me married to the Pope. Now let's satisfy this whim of yours: Hide behind the jasmines and the myrtles that serve as hedges for her garden. There, if you don't make too much noise, you'll get your heart's fill of her.

ANTONIO: Is there a painter in Avero?

JUANA: The Duke has some famous ones, but why do you ask?

ANTONIO: I wish to bring one here to paint a portrait of my beautiful Serafina. He could easily make a sketch of her as she puts on her costume.

JUANA: And what if Serafina hears of this or the painter lets people know of it?

ANTONIO: Money can harness tongues or let them loose. Either slay me or don't hinder me in this desire.

JUANA: You rush me so that I wish I'd remained silent or you'd never heard about her. Well, Cousin, you can see that I must love you if I do all this for you. Look for a painter without a tongue, and you won't choose wrong or your plans miscarry. Judging from all the different whims you exhibit, I'd guess that you were big with child. (Exeunt both.)

[The palace garden.]

(Enter the Duke and Madalena.)

DUKE: Daughter, if it is right to make me happy, then don't go on in this fashion; seeing you so joyless is as death to me. Heaven has given you a husband to make you happy, and the prospect of marriage to the Count of Vasconcelos does not deserve such a reaction. His father, the Duke of Berganza, has written you, and you should answer him. Write to the Count also, and don't let me see you so downcast or moody, lest in your melancholy you seek to cut short the days of my old age.

MADALENA: I'll seek to end my gloominess, so as not to sadden you, if the melancholy of one can truly sadden another. I'll strive to please you, but now, I wish to ask you one more small favor to add to the many you've already granted me.

DUKE: Go ahead, ask, but on the condition that you banish this sadness.

MADALENA (aside): *Love has seized my honor and sent it hurtling.* The prisoner freed at my request now depends completely on my favor. By this one act, my lord, it seems I have obligated myself. So, with your help, I have taken his elevation on myself. He's a fellow of fine appearance and wields a graceful pen.

DUKE: In brief, tell me what he wants.

MADALENA: He seeks to assume the post of your secretary.

DUKE: A short time ago—fifteen minutes in fact—I could have given it to him, but it was just filled.

MADALENA (aside): *Oh, love's folly. What nice work you've done now. Your weakness, coming to his aid too late, has spoiled everything. Though love has wings, it cannot fly.*

DUKE: On the direction of my steward, I have taken on a young man just come from Lisbon to Avero. From what I have seen of him, he shows himself to be clever and able.

MADALENA: My lord, I gave him my word and he is in hopes I'll assist him. Since my pen is so weak could he perhaps—unless you object— stay at the palace and assist me in writing to the Count and the Duke of Berganza. After all, it is a great deficiency in a woman of my station to write badly or be unable to compose or answer a letter. Some lessons from him, and I'll have a clearer hand.

DUKE: Enough. Let him tutor you and teach you to correct the blurs on your pages. At least with that exercise you will be distracted from your sorrows, which come from the vice of idleness. He can be your secretary.

MADALENA: Let me kiss your hands.

(Enter Count Don Duarte.)

COUNT: My lord...

The Timid Young Man at the Palace Gate

DUKE: Count Don Duarte!
COUNT: I come to you filled with joy.
DUKE: And what is the occasion of this happiness?
COUNT: The King enthusiastically receives my request to marry and has written you to that effect. His Majesty says that he would be pleased if I should choose your lordship's daughter to grace my home, and that from now on he will take care to show me his favor.
DUKE: This brings me happiness; to call you son is a source of joy for me. You must conceal this until Serafina warms to this change in condition. For, as you may know, she takes badly to the idea of marriage now.
COUNT: My adoring soul will be a model of patience.
DUKE: I'll do all that I may to intercede with her for you. But for now abandon your concerns. The Count of Vasconcelos will come soon and then I'll celebrate both weddings together.
COUNT: Waiting is painful.
DUKE: Madalena, don't be melancholy.
MADALENA: Sir, to please you is my source of joy.
DUKE: Let's see what the King writes.
COUNT: As the adage tells us, to wait, as to live, demands we be patient.
(Exeunt all but Madalena.)
MADALENA: With good reason love is called a sickness and madness. Like some who are ill, those in love manage to find a way to worsen. Now within the gates of my honor is the man who engages it in battle. Before long he will pillage my heart. This is only natural, for when someone looks for trouble, he is sure to trip over it. Portia swallowed fiery coals and then died. What then shall I do, having swallowed the fire of my passion to silence myself? I shall tell him then, not in words but by visible signs, of the unbearable torments I endure by my silence. For, as everyone knows, to be a woman and to be silent is not possible.

(Enter Juana, Antonio, and a painter.)

JUANA: From behind these myrtles and jasmines you can spy on your beloved. Be silent, and then your love will flourish.
ANTONIO: I already know that my seraph is the angel of this paradise, but if she should hear me, I will be Adam cast out from it.

JUANA: I'll have her rehearse the role facing the artist, allowing him to paint her with ease. Right now she's donning the male costume she insists on wearing. I'll go and let her know the garden is now closed and quiet. Cousin, good-bye. (Exit.)

ANTONIO: We are both artists, you and I: I've already made a portrait, one I love and which consumes me.

PAINTER: I can't quite catch your meaning.

ANTONIO: On the mind is impressed a miniature the artist employs prior to executing the actual painting. The mind is like a *tabula rasa*, as Aristotle called it, subject to a thousand images.

PAINTER: So the Philosopher says.

ANTONIO: Colors and tints form the image of the object, which the eyes look at and send to the Common Sense. That is the workshop where the mind contemplates things, but only in the form of outlines, until Understanding, the mirror that, with its different lights, clarifies all, illuminates all, and paints them. Once painted, Understanding offers them up for sale to that queen of fine taste and ideas, the Will, she who loves the good, whether it is real or apparent, as long as it is not unknown, for that which is not known is never loved by her.

PAINTER: This knowledge you get from Aristotle.

ANTONIO: She draws to herself all these canvasses, and, after unfolding them, selects and buys one or two, sometimes well and other times badly. Then she surrounds them with the frame of love and is made happy by them. She hangs them in the memory, which is where she keeps her most valued treasures. In the same way I glanced on the wondrous beauty of Doña Serafina. I took a tiny brush and made a sketch, and then my affections purchased it. After my thoughts adorned the work, they brought it to the memory. When the artist saw how well it turned out, he wrote on the bottom, *Amor me fecit*. Do you see now how one who loves paints?

PAINTER: Possessing a portrait already, why have you brought me here?

ANTONIO: Mine is a spiritual portrait, for, as you know, the affections are only spirit.

PAINTER: Well?

ANTONIO: Sight, which is a physical faculty, wants from your artist's

The Timid Young Man at the Palace Gate

skill a physical portrait, so that I can contemplate her beauty when I am alone.

PAINTER: No philosophy can match that of a man in love.

ANTONIO: I have an advanced degree in love. But hush, here comes my joy.

(Enter Doña Serafina, dressed in black as a man, and Doña Juana.)

JUANA: Are you really going to do this? Doesn't it disturb you to see yourself like this?

SERAFINA: It's common for women to wear costumes at Shrovetide. I seek to entertain myself in this way. You shouldn't be surprised that I wish to dress as a man, since nature has denied me the opportunity to be one.

JUANA: You so look like a man that I am falling in love with you. Finally, this is to take place tonight?

SERAFINA: Yes.

JUANA: I'd be more pleased if you entertained yourself in some other way than acting.

SERAFINA: Nothing can equal the many pleasures for all the senses to be found in playacting.

JUANA: Oh?

SERAFINA: What satisfaction is to be found in a celebration or a game that you can't discover in the theater? Doesn't the theater offer pleasure and present a thousand gifts that make you forget your troubles? Is not the ear entertained by its music? The clever fellow enjoys its wit and subtlety, the jolly man finds laughter, the gloomy one discovers sorrow, the sharp one encounters biting wit. Doesn't the stubborn fellow get a warning and the ignorant one a lesson? And doesn't the bravo find wars, and the prudent counsel? If you want to see Moors, there are Moors; if you crave tournaments, there you can find them; if bulls, a bullfight.

These are some of the epithets I've found best to describe the drama: copy of life, food of the wits, beloved lady of the intellect, banquet of the senses, bouquet of different tastes, sphere of the mind, Lethe washing away sorrows, and, finally, a delicacy, that, bought at different prices, starves the foolish and satisfies the wise. To which of these two groups do you aspire?

JUANA: I wish to follow the wise. A little farce would be a source of joy.

SERAFINA: Then what harm do you see in our presentation?

JUANA: Only that you appear in it.

SERAFINA: But why, if only my sister and her ladies will see it? Truly, your whimsy astonishes me.

ANTONIO: Listening to her wit, I'm spellbound. Begin drawing her, if any living hand can copy the singular beauty of seraphim!

PAINTER: She's human enough. I'll have no trouble.

ANTONIO: Doesn't the supreme sight of her leave you in a state of awe?

SERAFINA: The glass, Juana. I must make myself up.

JUANA: (Brings her a mirror.) Best be careful, my lady, lest, looking at yourself, you fall in love.

SERAFINA: Am I so beautiful like this?

JUANA: You may prove another Narcissus.

SERAFINA: Fine. I want to push back my hair this way so that when I remove my hat I will no longer appear to be a woman. Put the mirror here. Why do you move from one side to the other?

JUANA: In that way I impede the view of the artist hidden in the garden painting your portrait.

SERAFINA: What are you saying?

PAINTER: My God, this woman is giving us away. If the Duke should get wind of this, we're both in for it.

SERAFINA: In the garden there's a painter?

JUANA: Let him paint your portrait.

ANTONIO: What madness is this?

SERAFINA: Who'd dare such a thing?

JUANA: No one less than Aphrodite herself. Enraptured by you, she hides to paint your portrait.

ANTONIO: That's better.

JUANA (aside): *I wonder how he reacted to that.*

SERAFINA: How whimsical you are this afternoon.

PAINTER: When I paint her, would she be in female dress or as she is now?

ANTONIO: As she is. Let the world be astonished that a seraph should don the costume of a man.

PAINTER: The sketch is done; the rest I'll do at home.

SERAFINA: I'm done combing my hair; you can put the mirror away. Is my hair appealing this way? How do I look to you?

JUANA: Just like the handsome Medoro whom Angelica fell in love with in *Orlando Furioso*.

SERAFINA: But I'm not dressed like a Moor.

JUANA: No, but you are even more comely.

SERAFINA: Now that I am dressed like a man, let's rehearse the part.

JUANA: And what is the title of this piece?

SERAFINA: *The Cruel Lady of Portugal.*

JUANA: With such a title, the poet must have had you in mind.

SERAFINA: Portuguese I am, not cruel.

JUANA: But who can turn her back on love and not be cruel?

SERAFINA (donning her ruff, cloak, and hat): Is one cruel simply because she does not love? Tell me.

JUANA: Isn't it obvious?

SERAFINA: Would it be right to pity others and be cruel to myself?

PAINTER: By God, she has a golden tongue.

ANTONIO: Yes, but pity the wretch who hears that argument.

PAINTER: Be patient.

ANTONIO: If only my torments would allow me.

SERAFINA: Stop all this, and let me rehearse. You'll see how I act the part of a jealous man.

JUANA: What role do you play?

SERAFINA: A stupendous one—of a jealous prince who challenges a count on the field of honor.

JUANA: Go ahead.

SERAFINA: Though I am a stranger to jealousy, I can feign it.

(In her role of jealous lover): *Your unlimited boldness frees me from that honorable tolerance to which I am bound. By God, the behavior of you and the beautiful Celia astounds me—you for loving and speaking to her, she for lending an ear to your mad passion. Given the difference in our station, your base traits, this act has been one of disrespect.*

> *Listen: There can be no apology for such actions, and don't think words will substitute for a clumsy sword. Show some courage and let my suspicions come to an end, for it is degrading to be made jealous by a coward.* (She grasps her sword.) *Show your valor now; faint-hearted, base enemy, die.*

JUANA: Contain yourself! I am not the source of these troubles.

SERAFINA: How does it seem to you?

JUANA: It frightened me.

SERAFINA: I was enraged.

JUANA: If this angers you so, what would you do if you were really jealous?

ANTONIO: Has jealousy ever worn such a lovely face?

PAINTER: What a curious charm she possesses! Seeing her drives me to madness.

JUANA: Seeing you, I feared for a moment some misfortune could take place. A fine bravo you made.

SERAFINA: Now listen: Satisfied with the innocence of my beloved and her love for me, I tenderly entreat her forgiveness for my rage.

JUANA: This will be fine. Proceed.

SERAFINA (Acting): *As God is my witness, my offense to you reached to my very soul. There will be no more outbursts, I will punish myself. My darling, let us be as one. Shed that frown, and let the pupils of your eyes once again be my playmates. My glory, my light, my heaven, my consolation, my darling, this disdain of yours serves no end. Why turn your face from me? If my plea is not enough for you, then take this dagger— but no, you won't slay me, for despite your anger your feelings belong to me. So, Celia, let us end all this—be careful now, lest I be the angry one.* (She tries to embrace Doña Juana.) *Is it not my right? Don't go away, don't separate yourself from me.*

ANTONIO: The lucky man to hear such a thing.

JUANA: Slow, now. I fear you are melting, turning from snow to wax. 'Til this moment you've never been a true Portuguese woman. Tell me, my lady, can someone act and feel like a lover who does not love?

SERAFINA: I have not as yet experienced this mishap—one that offers more pain than profit. Now listen to these lines: You'll see how well I act the madman.

The Timid Young Man at the Palace Gate

(Acting) *So Celia is to wed the Count and I am to be forgotten! Heavens, change and women are both guided by the same star! What has become of those favors that were to be like flowers blooming into the fruits of my hopes? They were flowers indeed—the early blossoming flowers of almonds, dried up by a cold wind. I'm mad and would end my life. My mind is gone, and so let me lose my life too. But no, I'll go to their peasant wedding celebrating their peasant love. Yes, I'll go—after all if I'm the one to pay the bill, I may as well enjoy it, flying there on the fiery wings of jealousy. This has been just the right time to come. I can see her now— now as the guests emerge, one-two-three to the beat of a drum, all dancing to its rhythm. Since they're dancing, so will I.* (Serafina dances.) *One, two, three. Like the steps of the dance, I change my mind, since Celia was quick enough to change hers? Let the old man play; after all, the village has paid for it. Now they're inside for a wedding snack.* (She puts her cloak over her.) *With my cape I'll cover up my suffering. I'll hunch up in this corner, the perfect spot for me. They're serving hazelnuts and chickpeas to everyone...*

"Hey there, fool, over here, I'll take a handful."

"Me, a fool, liar!"

"Me, a liar. Take that." (Serafina slaps herself.)

"Slapped me, will you. You'll die for this!" (She draws a sword.)

"Hold it! What's happening here?"

"Stop it. What is this?" "It was nothing."

"Then let us be friends."

"Yes, let's. That's what I want to be." (Sheathing her sword.)

Now the priest has arrived.

"May this house rejoice with weddings for many a fine year."

"Thanks be to you, Father. Here, take a seat—not that one, the chair with a back."

"No, I won't."

"I say you must."

"This bench would have suited me ... but, rather than be stubborn..."

Now with the old fellow settled comfortably in his seat,

"Hernan Alonso, pour the wine and let the good Father have some and pass it around."

"The wine is soured with the taste of pitch."

...as Celia is of jealousy.

"Now is the time for them to pledge their troths..."
All are standing, the couple and their sponsors facing, and the priest in the middle of them.
"Fabio, do you take the beautiful Celia as your wife?"
"Yes, I do."
"Do you, Celia, take Fabio?"
"I take him for my husband and master."
(Draws a sword.) *"You pack of dogs! Right here in front of me. I am the Prince Pinabelo—let all of you die, the priest, the people."*
"Oh, he's killing us."
"Destroy them. Let them be consumed in the conflagration of my jealousy. If I'm now Samson, let Samson die with the Philistines, for no one can endure the fire ignited by love and blown by the winds of jealousy."

JUANA: Hold! Don't strike down this poor sinner! I'm not Celia, nor Celio either, so you've no reason to be angry with me.

SERAFINA: God's truth, I just exploded, carried away like Alexander hearing the court musician.

ANTONIO: Could heaven have joined more grace and charm in one person, even one of her quality? At the cost of his life, blessed is the man who gets to pour out his thoughts to her.

JUANA: You are skillful. You say the passage well.

SERAFINA: Doña Juana, come, I want to put my clothes on over this costume until it's time to put on the play.

JUANA: Surely this will offer an agreeable distraction to your despondent sister.

SERAFINA: I wish to amuse her. (Exeunt both women.)

PAINTER: They're gone.

ANTONIO: She's gone and I'm left here sad and blinded.

PAINTER: So, finally, you want me to paint her as a man?

ANTONIO: Yes, I wish to look at what she's worn and muse about what we've just seen. No ... change the suit.

PAINTER: No longer black?

ANTONIO: That would drape my hopes in mourning. Let it be the color of the sky tinged with gold; the blue, a traditional color of jealousy, gold of my love.

The Timid Young Man at the Palace Gate

PAINTER: It will be as you wish.

ANTONIO: But when can you have it done?

PAINTER: By tomorrow without fail.

ANTONIO: Ignore the cost. No one pierced by naked Cupid's arrow can keep his eye on his purse. (Exeunt Painter and Antonio.)

(Enter Madalena and Mireno.)

MADALENA: As of today, you are my teacher.

MIRENO: What could Your Grace have seen in me that would make you exalt me in this way? Starting today, the pupil will give the master a lesson.

MADALENA (aside): *What clear signs I give him of my blind love.*

MIRENO (aside): *How can I doubt what I have hoped has come true? Isn't this a show of love for me? All her favors express it, and this patronage shows it. Why does my shyness obstruct the chance heaven has bestowed? Show her you understand.*

MADALENA: Don Dionís, because I have so much love for...

MIRENO (aside): *Now, here it comes, her declaration of love. Heavens, she's about to say she loves me.*

MADALENA: ...for the Count of Vasconcelos. Before he arrives, I want to write not just with a more attractive hand but with the words piercing my heart. Inexperienced in love, I must ask you to instruct me how to declare what love commands and so weighs down my heart. I can scarce express my love, though I abound in it. I think you skilled in all things; you, my teacher, must teach me to write the Count and declare my love to him.

MIRENO (aside): *My grandiose illusions have deceived me. I am no more than a go-between for her with the Count. My mad fantasies have built towers in the air; without a base they fall to the ground. I have been like the ass bearing a statue of Isis during a village fair. In his vain madness he thought all the reverential displays were for him and tried with his animal impatience to toss off the statue until he was punished and calmed down and saw the truth. Her favor is the donkey's adoration. That's enough—no more will I be the ass! Only the Count is the statue. I can cease my courtly ways now. The feast is not for me.*

MADALENA (aside): *Fearing I was too forward, now I have turned his mind into a whirligig of confusion.* Tomorrow, teacher, we will begin our lessons.

MIRENO: To serve you is my sole wish.

MADALENA: You seem downcast.

MIRENO: Do I?

MADALENA: What troubles you?

MIRENO: Nothing.

MADALENA (aside): *Now I must give him some token of my feeling here.*

(She stumbles, extending her hand to him.)

O, my goodness, I tripped.... (aside) *For love always stumbles.* My heel twisted and I tripped.

MIRENO (aside): *Heavens! What blessing is this?* My lady, have you hurt yourself?

MADALENA: No, I don't think so.

MIRENO: But I grasped your hand...

MADALENA: Don't you know in court the lady who gives a man her hand also gives him a foothold? (Exit Madalena.)

MIRENO: "...in court the lady who gives a man her hand also gives him a foothold." What can I make of all this? Would my vain thoughts tell me if I'm winning or losing? What sort of confusion and worry is this? Heaven, tell me, isn't this love? But no it's not—I'm just carrying the statue of the Count of Vasconcelos. If so, what is all this business about a hand and a foothold? What can I expect if she loves the Count? If only my lady would tell me why she persists in constructing this maze! All these confusions spin around my brain—suspicions, love—she loves me, she loves me not? No! I'm just carrying the statue of the Count of Vasconcelos. All I can expect is that for her next lesson I'll teach her how to express the passion the Count has stirred. There's nothing for me but to endure and in my shame stay silent. My ambition has had enough daring flights raised by foolish thoughts to the heavens. For I am nothing but the bearer of the statue of the Count of Vasconcelos.

ACT III

[A shepherd's home.]

(Enter Lauro, an old shepherd, and Ruy Lorenzo in shepherd dress.)

The Timid Young Man at the Palace Gate

RUY: If age and prudence furnish patience in adversity, then, wise Lauro, let your years and your prudence withstand this trial. Leave off your never-ending weeping. If the absence of your son is the source of this flood of tears, know that your lament will soon turn to rejoicing, for virtue was always the basis of good fortune, and since virtue has always been as a mother to him, this will be the beginning of good fortune.

LAURO: My ill fortune insists I weep, for I know that sons must inherit the afflictions of their fathers. In my old age he was to be the wall separating me from unhappiness, but, alas, my sole legacy to him is my misery.

RUY: Is this wisdom? If you weep for the troubles that beset you, what of a man such as I? Heaven has taken away my honor, my country, and my name. Yours is but the loss of a son, and you haven't lost hope of enjoying the sight of him again. But when shall I see an end to the reversals in my life, those you know all too well? Will the rage of this cruel time ever cease and I be able to shed this costume and the name of traitor? You must console me, for mine is the greater loss.

LAURO: Have you lost more than a son?

RUY: Is not honor more than life or sons?

LAURO: Yes.

RUY: Then, without hope of restoring my honor, I have lost more.

LAURO: It is you who tainted your vengeance, for vengeance must be within the bounds of honor. Seeking to restore honor by dishonorable means only brings greater dishonor. You should have sought some other way than forging the signature and stamp of the Duke to kill the Count. If these hostile times seem a punishment to you, find comfort in the knowledge that you suffer for your guilt—my punishment is undeserved.

RUY: An absent son is no great injury.

LAURO: Let me recount the misfortunes I've endured all these years despite my innocence. Perhaps the injuries done to another will make yours seem less.

RUY: Men of noble and generous spirit do not hold with such a notion. The wise and astute man feels the sufferings of another as his own.

LAURO: If you guard my secret, my tears will relate my story.

RUY: I promise. Still, to weep over a missing son is weakness in a man. If you had my miseries, how much greater would be your grief.

LAURO: With his loss I've lost more than just a son. Oh heavens! If you knew who I am, how small would seem your misfortunes.

RUY: What does this puzzle mean?

LAURO: Since you wear my son's clothes, listen to the account of his father's misfortunes. Ruy, I was not born to this harsh life, nor to these coarse clothes, my name is not Lauro, this mountain range is not my home. Nor did those of my noble blood ever cultivate the soil. My name is Don Pedro of Portugal. I come in direct descent from the kings of Portugal. The King, Don Duarte, was my brother, and the present ruler is my nephew.

RUY: What am I hearing? Then you must be the Duke of Coimbra. Let me fall down before you and be silent about my misfortunes—for, besides yours, they are tiny, invisible even.

LAURO: Rise, and if you have the patience, listen to discover how fortune's wheel turns. The King of Portugal, my brother, died in the springtime of his life, but then what is not withered by death? With his death the Queen and I became guardians of the kingdom and his son, then six years of age, now a man who seeks to end my life and honor. The Queen and I differed over how the country should be ruled, for pride never learned to admit company, and tongues of envious flatterers will always sow dissension. The King of Castile, the brother of the Queen, intervened, deciding that she and I each should rule half the kingdom and she be guardian of the Prince. I accepted this agreement, but it did not put an end to envy and suspicion. The kingdom became roiled and seemed to be on the verge of armed conflict. All this ceased when death brought an end to the beautiful Queen's ambition. Then I ruled Portugal without competition until Alfonso the Fifth was old and strong enough. To him I married my daughter, Isabella, given me by heaven, whom he neither respected nor appreciated. A thousand flatterers gathered around the King, and, as is the custom with such men, they closed off the palace doors to truth. One of them, a commoner named Vasco Fernández, sought to secure his position by striking me down from mine. To this end he persuaded my own brother that I planned to seize his lands and meet him in battle at Berganza, where, through my efforts, he was Duke. Both men then told the King that to gain power I had, along with other acts of treason, poisoned his mother. They convinced

The Timid Young Man at the Palace Gate

him I was plotting to seize his kingdom, persuading him by the use of forged letters to the English King. They convinced him that to rule in safety he would have to imprison me. Believing all this, he took away my lands and the wealth I had gained while governing. Removing me to the castle fort, despite the tears and entreaties of my daughter, his wife, Isabella, he ordered his men to take off my head. When I discovered the punishment planned for me, I told my wife and, propelled by fear, tied sheets together and lowered myself from my cell down the prison's wall.

Learning of my escape, the King ordered that, at the sound of blaring trumpets, I be proclaimed a traitor, and gave license my life be taken, prescribing mortal punishment to anyone who knew my whereabouts without revealing them. Fearing the cruelty of such an order, and not wanting to test the loyalty of my friends, we came to these mountains. I bought some land and sheep, and from a duke I became a shepherd. Here, from sadness and childbirth, my beloved wife died, leaving me a beautiful son, who grew up in peasant's clothes.

For twenty years springs have brought flowers to May, grass to the meadows, and sorrows to me, as you see me now. All of that would be nothing but for the loss of my son, in whose presence my troubles were naught. Now, is it not reasonable for me in my old age to be so grieved by the loss of him, to die perhaps amid a flood of tears?

RUY: The scenes which time, that venerable and mad author of so many tragedies, presents on the world's stage, are remarkable indeed. Your sufferings, illustrious Duke, make me forget my own: But I hope to God that fortune will soon turn around. Your son's bearing, hidden beneath his coarse coat like cinders from the flames of his nobility, emitted powerful signs of his true rank. Please God heaven return him to you a prosperous man, a fount of consolation.

(Enter Vasco and Bato, shepherds.)

BATO: Master, we're on our way to Avero with five wagons of firewood. Do you want something there?

LAURO: Only your prompt return.

BATO: Nothing else?

LAURO: No.

BATO: But I do: Using my wages as credit, will you give me enough cash for a pretty hat Firela wants?

LAURO: Come here and take them.

BATO: I've noted all of this on my tally stick; besides this, I owe you just five more marvedis.

LAURO: What simplicity! (Exeunt Bato and Lauro.)

VASCO: May I go as well?

RUY: No, my friend, unless you never intend to come back. You know of the dangers and charges we face.

VASCO: And for how long must I wander along this vulgar path clothed in this base costume, exiled from my breeches? Let me return to them and save me from a mastiff who took a half pound out of my leg last night in front of Melisa's door.

RUY: And what were you doing at her door during the night?

VASCO: Yesterday she showed me a sign of her affection: With all her strength, she gave me the most almighty pinch in the arm and winked with her left eye.

RUY: This is a sweet token?

VASCO: Isn't it clear? This is the mark of love in country villages. (Exeunt both of them.)

[A room in the palace.]

(Enter Mireno and Tarso.)

TARSO: What more could you ask as a sign of love than for her to say, "in court the lady who gives a man her hand also gives him a foothold"? Can a woman of rank say it more clearly? What are you waiting for? You're what I'd call a stingy and bashful lover, since you dare not be bold. Are you waiting for the woman to perform the man's role? In what species isn't the female courted, pursued, and wooed? Start courting her; to do anything else is to break the perfect order created by nature. Speak: Don't lose such a fine and high-ranking woman by your silence.

MIRENO: Tarso, I find myself in a labyrinth of fear and doubt. I can't see how heaven would give its blessings to me rather than to the Count. Look at a comparison between us: on the one hand, a great noble, a clever fellow, and on the other, a humble one from a shepherd's background, a base branch of a poor trunk. I can't see the heavens selecting me. How could so noble a woman favor copper over gold? I have made

The Timid Young Man at the Palace Gate

a catalog of the favorable signs she has shown me: her friendly speech, her uncertain expression, the way she looks at me, her puzzling and roundabout explanations of her wishes, her feigned fall (if it was feigned), her extension to me of her hand and her confused expression. All this leaves me perplexed, on a strand between fear and hope. Now, when I burn to speak to her, shyness holds me back and covers my mouth.

TARSO: Shyness! Can a man utter such a word? I rage to hear such a stupid thing—and with good reason! It should come as no surprise if I call your fear plain insanity. Oh what a poor creature you are. Or are you the shy maiden whose slowness to act cries out bashfulness? I'm sure I don't know why a timid young man would try to enter the palace gate. A love that is timid and silent will come to naught. If Cupid were a shy fellow, he wouldn't be painted naked! Don't be afraid she may lash out at you when you tell her how you feel: Put a fold over your eyes, not your mouth. Talk to her—or I will. If you are silent, she who would give you a foothold will leave you with nothing.

MIRENO: Now, Brito, I see that a silent love makes no sense. But what if I lose by speaking what she has given me already—patronage and the enduring if insane hope of her love? What if declaring my passion produces only punishment and disappointment? Isn't it reasonable to hold onto a doubtful love with a silent tongue rather than to endure certain disdain? This is the point of my shyness, the aim of my secrecy.

TARSO: A wise man once said that there are three situations in which fear and shyness are bad: in the pulpit, in the palace, and in love. You are in the palace, and heaven has opened a wide road for you. Don't let your shyness make you lose your way.

MIRENO: How can this be if she loves the Count of Vasconcelos?

TARSO: Don't believe it.

MIRENO: But if I see it and she says it…

TARSO: It's a dodge and a scheme to find out if you love her. Open your heart to her. If she doesn't respond, we can return to the mountains in time for the harvest.

MIRENO: If I'm not kept back by my shyness, I'll do it, even if I lose my reputation and my life.

(Enter Doña Juana.)

JUANA: Don Dionís, my mistress is calling you.
MIRENO: I will go right away.
TARSO: Courage.
MIRENO (aside): *What is this intimidating confusion that holds me back?*
JUANA: Come quickly. She's waiting for you. (Exit Juana.)
TARSO: Unfold your heart. Speak calmly to her.
MIRENO: I tremble, Brito.
TARSO: That can't be helped. Whoever said it was the Devil who brought the timid young man to the palace gate hit the mark. (Exeunt Tarso and Mireno.)

[The apartment of Doña Madalena.]

(Enter Doña Madalena.)

MADALENA: Cupid, how can fear and shame restrain you? If you really dwell in him and he calls you his god, why do his fears hold back his love from me? How can a man be so timid? So silent? Let him declare his passion to me, for such reticence does not become a man. Just once let his tongue utter what his eyes exclaim. And if the differences in our stations make him fearful, surely my daring liberties have given him the chance to speak and to act.

Haven't my eyes already told him of my love, though in vain? When I gave him my hand. my love was in it, and my tongue was not silent either, even at the expense of propriety. As much as modesty permits, I have opened the door to my love. Cupid, why did you give me a lover who was mute?

But, humbled as I am, his silence should not surprise me; even if I told him of my love, he probably wouldn't believe me.

(Enter Doña Juana.)

JUANA: My lady, Don Dionís has come to give you a lesson. (Exit Juana.)
MADALENA: Since he hasn't any words for me, he will have to give me a lesson in how to be silent. But love so abuses me that my pain will not consent for me to hold my tongue. I will openly declare my love to him, contrary to custom and order—but in a way that, though I tell him everything, still he will be unsure. (She sits in a chair and pretends to sleep.)

The Timid Young Man at the Palace Gate

(Mireno enters.)

MIRENO: What does your ladyship command of me? Is it time for a lesson? (aside) *Now in her presence, I start to tremble. She hasn't seen me yet, as she is silent, seated on the chair, her hand on her cheek. She's silent, perhaps she's not yet seen me.*

MADALENA (aside): *Any resistance is useless. I'll express my love as if I'm dreaming.*

MIRENO: My lady, it is I, Dionís. She doesn't respond. Yes, she is sleeping. Now is the time for daring; go ahead and allow yourself to contemplate the beauty that clouds your understanding. With her eyes closed you can approach without fear, for even if the eyes are the shafts of love, they can't wound you now.

Did the Supreme Creator of our nature make a more polished beauty? To kiss her hand is my desire. Shall I, yes ... but no ... it is a divine relic, and my lowly mouth unworthy to touch it. But can I call myself a man and still tremble? What is this? Courage, well, isn't she asleep? Yes. I'll go to her. (He approaches and then withdraws.) I'll go. What if she should waken? Good Lord, the danger is obvious, and I'll die if she awakens and finds me like this. Better I lose this little bit than throw away everything. Let my fear conquer my love. It's best to wait outside.

MADALENA (aside): *He didn't even dare come near me. Curse his shyness!*

MIRENO: To be alone here with her asleep seems improper. I'll go now.

MADALENA (aside): *Is he going away after all?*

(All Madalena's speeches in this exchange
are spoken as if talking in her sleep.)

Don Dionís...

MIRENO: Did she call me? Yes. How quickly she awakened. Consider my dilemma if I'd given in to my impulse. Is she awake? But no. My long-delayed hopes will come to fruition in her dreams. And someone who cares for me when she's asleep cannot disdain me awake. Maybe she's dreaming of me right now! Oh heavens! If I could only know what's in her mind.

MADALENA (as if talking in her sleep): Don Dionís, don't go away, come closer, over here.

MIRENO: In her dreams she commands I approach. What a happy chance! To obey her is only right, for even in her sleep she is still my mistress. Love, say what you will, and leave shyness behind.

MADALENA: You've come to give me lessons both in writing and in love ... to the Count of Vasconcelos...

MIRENO: Oh what am I seeing through my jealous eyes?

MADALENA: I'd like to see if you know what love and jealousy are—to teach what you don't know would be a serious failing.

Tell me, are you in love? Are you blushing? What shame has overtaken you? Give me an answer; rid yourself of your fears. Don't you know that love is a tribute, a natural debt of all who live, from the lowest beasts to angels?

(Still feigning sleep, she then asks and answers her own questions.)

"If this is true, why are you so embarrassed? Are you very much in love"?

"Yes, my lady, I am."

(aside) *Well, thank God, at last I got a word out of him.*

MIRENO: Could she be dreaming of love? What a lucky man I am to hear and contemplate this, though you'd think I was the one dreaming—if I am, let me not awaken.

MADALENA (she continues questioning and answering):

"Have you told the lady that you love yet?"

"I haven't dared."

"Then she doesn't know of it?"

"Since love is all fire and flames, for sure she will have observed it just by looking at my adoring eyes silently cry it out."

"This task must be done by the tongue, for the language of lovers is not clearly understood. Indeed, some call it gibberish. Hasn't she given you the opportunity to declare yourself?"

"So many times that I am amazed by my timidity."

"Speak up then, for such hesitation does an injustice to your love."

"But I fear losing by speaking what I enjoy in silence."

"Nonsense! A wise man once compared a lover who is silent to a rolled-up Flemish painting. The artist profits little if he does not unfold his canvasses to display his wares. Shyness never finds welcome in a

The Timid Young Man at the Palace Gate

palace. Spread open that painting so it may be sold: The illness never spoken of is not easily cured."

"Yes, my lady, but our inequality holds me back."

"Isn't love a god?"

"Yes, my lady."

"Then speak, for its laws are absolute. They dethrone kings and make equal the shepherd's crook and the king's miter. I wish to intercede for you; tell me, who is it you love?"

"I dare not."

"What is it you fear? Do I make a bad intermediary?"

"No, but oh my goodness, I am afraid."

"Should I give you her name, will you say perhaps that I am she?"

"Yes, my lady."

"Now is the time for me to be silent, and you to speak. I suppose I know what's causing this, you are jealous of the Count."

"My lady, he makes me despair that you will ever be mine, for, after all, he is your equal and heir to the House of Berganza."

"In love, equality and likeness are not a matter of wealth or poverty, high or low station, but in the conformity of the hearts and wills of two people. Henceforth, Don Dionís, make your feelings known. I exhort you to recall this: In games of love it's better to go beyond the limit than fall short of the mark. For some time now I have preferred you to the Count of Vasconcelos."

MIRENO: Sweet heaven, what is it I'm hearing?

(Madalena pretends to awaken at this last cry of Mireno.)

MADALENA: My Lord, who's here? Who brought you to me, Don Dionís?

MIRENO: My lady...

MADALENA: What are you doing here?

MIRENO: I came to give my lady a lesson. I found you asleep and I waited here for you to awaken.

MADALENA: I fell asleep, but I don't understand what could have happened to me. To be asleep like this is something new for me. (She rises.)

MIRENO: Oh what joy for me if you would always dream as you did just now.

MADALENA (aside): *Well at last this mute has finally spoken.*

MIRENO (aside): *I tremble all over.*
MADALENA: You know what I dreamt?
MIRENO: It was no great task to know that.
MADALENA: You must be another Joseph.
MIRENO: In shyness I have been his twin, but not in intuition.
MADALENA: Finish explaining to me how you know about my dream.
MIRENO: In your sleep you explained it all.
MADALENA: My Lord!
MIRENO: The sense of it, as best I could figure out, is a judgment in my favor, though if my happiness is to be sure, my lady must confirm it when she is awake.
MADALENA: I recall nothing—tell me about it, maybe something will come back.
MIRENO: My lady, I dare not.
MADALENA: If you do not dare to tell me, it must be bad indeed.
MIRENO: Nothing more wicked than you showing me your favor.
MADALENA: I very much wish to hear it. Finish this, now, by my life.
MIRENO: Such an oath inspires boldness: When your ladyship slept … no, I am too shy.
MADALENA: Don't be tiresome, Don Dionís, get to the point.
MIRENO: You openly showed your love for me.
MADALENA: I did? How?
MIRENO: You lifted the burden of my jealousy. Sleeping, you declared…
MADALENA: Yes?
MIRENO: That you prefer me over the Count of Vasconcelos, hardly an insignificant favor, you must admit.
MADALENA: Don't trust in dreams, Don Dionís, for dreams are just dreams. (Exit.)
MIRENO: That's what you leave me with? Just as my hopes rise, the weight of disdain puts the scale in perfect balance. Her stark expression dampens my joy. The passion here is as useless as a dull or chipped sword. Why does heaven guide love down so many different paths? I'm caught between the dark of her disdain and the light of her affection. This is it, now it's final: I'll never speak up again, since the woman asleep loved me but awake had nothing for me but scorn.

Let my heart be silent or find a better mistress to serve—and never, never again put faith in dreams, for dreams are nothing but dreams.

(Enter Tarso.)

TARSO: Well, sir, how did it go?

MIRENO: How should I know? Neither well, nor badly. Spread, like the two legs of a compass, I'm stuck, equally loved and disdained. From now on it's back to being cautious and shy. I've found they work better for me.

TARSO: So, the boat of love sailed without you?

MIRENO: Later on when we have more time we'll chat about this.

TARSO: Bato, your father's cowherd, is in Avero and caught sight of me. He's mad with joy that you're here and wants to see and talk to you.

MIRENO: And of course he will. Oh for my simple hamlet! How much better are its ways than those of this confusing palace where deception is the way of things! Brito, let's go and speak to Bato, and I'll write my father about my fortune and my situation. I'll see Bato in some isolated spot.

TARSO: Why?

MIRENO: Because my humble station will become known before this whole business gets sorted out.

TARSO: You've got a point there.

MIRENO: Let's be off and make Bato happy.

TARSO: We're both in a confused mess—you for love, me for these breeches. (Exeunt Tarso and Mireno.)

[Serafina's rooms.]

(Enter Doña Serafina and Antonio.)

SERAFINA: Count, I haven't decided whether or not to inform my father of your rashness, a clear insult to him. Surely, as a noble, you could have found another way to meet the Duke without pretending to be his secretary. Unless you hold me in very low esteem, a woman of loose morals, it's beyond me how you could have dared such a thing.

ANTONIO: Travelling, I came to see my cousin when love beckoned me to stay.

SERAFINA: Count, that's enough! With just cause I take offense at your boldness. Did you believe that I hold my honor and reputation so cheap that, discovering this outrage, I'd submit to you? That you'd think me such an easy woman is an offense to my honor. My father has promised me to the Count of Estremoz, but even if I did not have the slightest interest in him, just to punish you for this act of madness, I would marry him. If you do not leave Avero immediately I'll inform Don Duarte; if he hears of it, your life is in peril, for he will deem this a serious insult.

ANTONIO: So you spurn me this way?

SERAFINA: Count, leave or I'll scream!

ANTONIO: Please, let me defend myself against these charges; even the severest judge allows the criminal to speak before being sentenced.

SERAFINA: For the love of heaven—be out of here within the hour, or, just to spite you, I'll marry the Count this very night! What can you want of me? Don't you see I don't love you? I can't even stand you. Indeed, the sight of you is the worst grief that could be inflicted on me. If your love is not requited, what is the point in loving me? Count, get away from me. (She moves away.)

ANTONIO: You are an asp hiding your venom within the rose of your beauty. Oh God, I burn in hell with no hope my suffering will ever lessen! Since you exile me from the paradise of your sight, may you be like Narcissus and love no one but yourself, consumed by your own image and beauty, and weep endlessly as I do.

As you insist, I'll go away, fleeing a stern cruelty that brings shame to all your sex. Banished from your sight, my hopes for happiness lost, I gain some satisfaction by exiling this image from my breast.

(He removes the portrait.)

Let my vengeance find solace in the sea of forgetfulness in which I drown myself. May at last the sea in which I sink be calmed—if it can, with waves of flames. Ingrate, let my heart erase the likeness love painted on it.

(He throws it on the ground.)

To cast this thing away is just punishment for my just anger towards the woman who so mistreats my love for her. Adieu, cruel portrait, tossed on the stony ground, the image of one so adamantine. Still, I

The Timid Young Man at the Palace Gate

have recourse to time, that wise physician who cures madness. Let the fire of my passion melt like snow in flames. (Exit Antonio.)

SERAFINA: What madness! Are all poor devils in love victims of such violent upheavals? How blessed I am not to have submitted myself to the yoke of such a cruel master! What is it that he flung on the ground excoriating my ingratitude? Let me look.

A portrait! (she picks it up) It's of a man, and it resembles me in every way. It's like looking in a burnished mirror, and yet a man is its subject.

My heavens, who is he? It in no way looks like the Count, so what's the point of throwing it at my feet? The object so bewitches me that it must be enchanted. Can a man look so like me? It makes no sense; even if there were one, what could this poor fellow have done to make the Count hate him so? If it were of me, then it would make sense.

There's some tangle here, something more than meets the eye here. What an odd business! I'll call his cousin Juana about it, even though we quarreled after I spied her hand in this affair. Here she is.

(Enter Doña Juana.)

JUANA: The garden is open; among the carnations and the jasmine will be a good place for you to spend some time and let cool your anger towards me.

SERAFINA: Doña Juana, look at this portrait.

JUANA (aside): *It's of her. Why did my cousin leave this here? God help me if she finds out I placed him in the garden.*

SERAFINA: Did you ever see such a likeness in your life?

JUANA: No, certainly I haven't. (aside) *It's the one the painter made in the garden.*

SERAFINA: Doesn't it surprise you?

JUANA: Very much.

SERAFINA: Your cousin reacted to my rejection of him with an angry fury. Screaming, leaving in a rage, he threw it on the ground. Picking it up to look at it, I was disturbed by its likeness to me, and must find out what all this has been about. Since you carry the keys to his heart, tell me if you know something.

JUANA (aside): *Thank God for the man's clothing and color or she'd realize she was the subject.* You ask me about something of which I am ignorant and astonished.

SERAFINA: I wish you knew something; I'd give a good deal to know who this is.

JUANA: ...to know about this?

SERAFINA: What?

JUANA: Just call my cousin back and ask some favor of him.

SERAFINA: Good idea—a fine scheme, but won't he have gone by now?

JUANA: Not yet; I'll go and call him.

SERAFINA: Go quickly.

JUANA (aside): *What an extraordinary thing!—heaven's just punishment: She who loves no one should fall in love with her own image.* (Exit.)

SERAFINA (looking at her portrait): Though the man who threw you on the ground was unkind, it will not be for naught: If the original is as comely as his copy, I promise I won't be unloving to him. He on canvass will achieve what flesh and blood could not. Still, no one should be surprised at my fickleness, for likeness has ever been the cause of love.

(Enter Don Antonio and Juana.)

JUANA (aside): *Yes, it's certain, she wants to see you.*

ANTONIO: What a confused mess this is.

JUANA (aside): *Watch how you answer her.*

ANTONIO (aside to Juana): *With a clever lie I'll seize my chance.*

SERAFINA: Count...

ANTONIO: My lady...

SERAFINA: You're quite angry.

ANTONIO: A common condition of the Portuguese, and besides, you gave me thirty minutes to be out of Avero. No wonder I raged like a loon.

SERAFINA: Hush. You don't know much about women. A woman's fury is like French horses—at first they gallop, then they tire. Time tames everything.

ANTONIO (aside to Juana): *This is all a ruse.*

SERAFINA: I don't want you to leave now.

ANTONIO: If that is so, I look at your past scorn of me as a blessing.

The Timid Young Man at the Palace Gate

SERAFINA: Now that you've calmed down, won't you tell me the reason why you threw this portrait on the ground as you left? What motive prompted something so unexpected? And tell me, whose portrait is this?

ANTONIO: I seek to tell you the truth, but I don't dare.

SERAFINA: But why?

ANTONIO: I fear a terrible punishment.

SERAFINA: You needn't fear anything. You have my word.

ANTONIO: Your presence gives me the heart to declare myself, and, besides, to give one's life for a friend is no great thing. (aside to Juana) *Now listen to this string of lies.*

SERAFINA: Well, go ahead.

ANTONIO: No doubt you know the long and sad story of the great Duke of Coimbra, the ruler of this kingdom who astonished all in peace and war. As he was kin to your father, the two of you must have wept over his misfortunes.

SERAFINA: Yes, my father recounted the whole sad story to Madalena and me, and the thought of it still moves me. I'd like to know where and if the Duke is still living.

ANTONIO: Only the Duchess is dead, though her memory endures. After the Duke escaped from prison, my father, at risk to himself, provided a refuge. Disguised in coarse coats the two, father and son, cultivate the land which they irrigate with their tears, though it yields nothing but thorns. Heaven has given the son many gifts—cleverness, bearing, gallantry—admired by all. Growing up together, he is half my soul. Six months ago he came to this hamlet, saw you, and lost his heart. Since then the valley echoes with his cry of love: "Serafina has slain me." A thousand times he vowed to tell you of his plaint, but stopped for fear that he, his father, and their protector would be denounced as traitors by the King, since the rigor of justice reaches everyone. The oceans of tears he cries for you I feel as if my own, and I pledged that one day I would declare his love to you, and give you the portrait of his dashing bearing and visage that is now in your hand. When I arrived and learned that your nature was a disdainful one, indisposed to yield to love's yoke, of which few are free, I did not dare declare openly the enigma of his amorous anguish until the right moment presented itself.

So that the Duke would receive me, I prevailed upon my cousin. When I discovered he intended for you to marry the Duke of Estremoz, I sought to prevent it with my feigned passion, which so angered you I threw the image at your feet, sure that the painted comeliness would quickly subdue your haughty conceit, which indeed it has. To be brief, the original of this image is Don Dionís de Coimbra.

SERAFINA: Count, is this true?

ANTONIO: Yes, it's true, and if he were here and knew you loved him, I believe he would come and give his heart to you, without concern of being discovered.

SERAFINA (aside): *If this is true, Don Duarte can no longer remain in my affections. My God, he's the son of Don Pedro!*

ANTONIO: His handsome appearance declares it!

SERAFINA (aside): *How frail I suddenly feel! I know that I'm not now the person I was. And how fitting that the man I love looks so like me. Couldn't I see him?*

ANTONIO: If you would put an end to your wrath, speak to him in the garden, where he will vault over the walls to be near you. But this must not be by day: Someone in Avero seems suspicious of him, and if this person sees him again ... well, you see the danger.

SERAFINA: Count, not to love a man who so corresponds to me in love and rank would be ingratitude. The discretion you've shown tells me I can trust you to arrange a meeting for us, for my heart begins to surrender its freedom to him, something it has long refused to do. Goodbye.

ANTONIO: You are leaving?

SERAFINA: I've said enough, for shame should speak little. (Exit.)

JUANA: Can this be—Don Pedro and his son still alive?

ANTONIO: Hush! I don't know a thing about the Duke or his family. With this clever ruse I plan to get what I seek. By night I'm Don Dionís, by day the Count of Penela.

JUANA: My cousin, you better know what you're doing.

ANTONIO: This deception allows love to come to me in the person of another, since by myself I can do nothing. (Exeunt Juana and Antonio.)

[Madalena's apartment.]

The Timid Young Man at the Palace Gate

(Enter the Duke and Madalena.)

DUKE: I was pleased with the line I saw on an envelope you sent to the Count, and would observe you getting a lesson. Already your writing is clearer.

MADALENA (aside): *Not so clear that Don Dionís couldn't misunderstand it and even take offense at it.*

(Enter Mireno.)

MIRENO: Did you call me, my lady?

MADALENA: My father wishes to see if my handwriting has improved, and you can tell us something about it, can't you?

MIRENO: Yes, my lady.

MADALENA: Not half an hour ago, half asleep I wrote a page so clear anybody would have understood even if he couldn't read. Don Dionís, do I make myself understood?

MIRENO: Quite well.

MADALENA: If it was good enough, it should prompt you to praise it.

MIRENO: I praise it with my silence. No matter how much I blame it on the pen, I find the last line so confusing it's not to my taste.

MADALENA: You say that because of the blot I made at the very end.

MIRENO: Yes, indeed.

MADALENA: But I put it there on purpose.

MIRENO: I only corrected the blot because it blurred everything else.

MADALENA: But you could erase it; besides, a blot is no disgrace.

MIRENO: What do you mean?

MADALENA (aside): *A slip of the tongue can be corrected, but not by staying silent.* Now then, sharpen a quill for me.

(He removes a pen from a portable writing table and sharpens the quill.)

MIRENO: My lady, I'm sharpening it now.

MADALENA (angry): Get on with it! You're slow getting to the point. Your Grace may conclude that this man's slowness prevents him from carrying out his proper task.

DUKE: I'm satisfied with everything concerning his penmanship.

MADALENA: It's no small matter having to explain something point by point and getting nowhere. Finish up please.

DUKE: Madalena, restrain yourself.

MIRENO: Do you want the nibs short?

MADALENA: You have a real fondness for shortness. No, I don't want them short of the mark! I want them long. Cut them that way or let them be!

MIRENO: Now, my lady, I've cut them.

DUKE: Madalena, how out of sorts you are.

MADALENA: A timid man who comes short of the mark can't help but be irksome.

MIRENO: The pen is sharpened now.

MADALENA: Show it to me. What a bad job! My Lord! (After using it, she throws it on the floor.)

DUKE: Why did you fling it on the floor?

MADALENA (to Mireno): You always give it to me with the fuzz on it. God keep me from you! Take them off with a knife. How you always leave feathers on the quill I'll never know. (aside) *And a bridle on your tongue.*

MIRENO (aside): *The heavens are smiling on me. This is all in my favor.*

(Enter Don Duarte.)

COUNT: My great lord, I bring joyous news: The Count of Vasconcelos is but a day from here.

MADALENA (aside): *Oh, my Lord.*

COUNT: He'll be here tomorrow, but the stay granted him means he'll only have time to wed and hurry back. I'll go and receive him while you make the necessary arrangements.

DUKE: Has he sent me some word?

COUNT: Here's a letter for you.

DUKE: My daughter, the moment I've looked forward to has at last arrived.

MADALENA (aside): *Don't depend on it.*

MIRENO (aside): *Oh my God!*

MADALENA (aside): *Oh, my lover sighs.*

The Timid Young Man at the Palace Gate

DUKE: Let us be off: Forget everything else but this: Tomorrow you will marry. (Exeunt the Duke and the Count. Madalena begins to write.)

MADALENA: Don Dionís, when I have finished writing here, read what I've written and do as it commands. (she writes)

MIRENO: If I've lost my chance, what shall I do? Can fate be so cruel!

MADALENA: In love, timing is everything. (Exit.)

MIRENO: She's gone now; let's see what she's written: "Do not delay: Tonight in the garden the fears of the timid young man at the palace gate will come to an end."

Good Lord! What did I just say? What did I read? Tonight? Can there be greater good fortune? Is this a dream? Am I mad? This can't be. I don't believe it. (He rereads the letter.) "Tonight in the garden..." My Lord, it's right here! I am blessed! Could there be a better ending? Soon in that flowery spot my jealousy will turn to love and then the Count of Vasconcelos will end up envying the timid young man at the palace gate. I've got to find Brito. (Exit.)

(Enter Lauro, Ruy Lorenzo, Bato, and Melisa.)

LAURO: May God give you His blessings. Bato, as a reward, choose the best sheep of the flock—no, one is too little, choose two. My son in Avero! My cousin the secretary of the Duke! Oh how capricious is time! But how can I complain now? Let's both be off and see him—how my eyes will sparkle at the sight of him. Come.

RUY: And what if I'm recognized?

LAURO: God wouldn't allow such a thing. Just smudge some soot on your face like a collier. Today my sad old age is taking a holiday in Avero. My joy grows by leaps and bounds. I feel as if I'm starting to live again. Enough talk. Ruy, let's be off.

BATO: We can all go together.

LAURO: No, stay and mind the house. (Exeunt Lauro and Ruy.)

MELISA: Let Beelzebub mind the house.

BATO: What's ailing you this afternoon?

MELISA: How should such a thing happen and Tarso not even ask for me?

BATO: He doesn't give a fig for you and he isn't Tarso.

MELISA: Then who is he?

BATO: Brito.

MELISA: How could he?! Right this afternoon I'm off to see this vicious swine!

BATO: By yourself?

MELISA: I'll take Vasco with me.

BATO: Well, you've got a good mastiff trailing you. Are you so mad about Tarso?

MELISA: Completely.

BATO: Well, he's changed once from Tarso to Brito. Once married he'll change again—from a man to a stag, horns and all. (Exeunt Bato and Melisa.)

[The Duke's garden at night.]

(Juana and Serafina at the window.)

SERAFINA: My sweet Juana! You know by this I risk my good name, but I can't delay. Tomorrow I'm to be married to the Duke.

JUANA: Even in the smallest way, Don Duarte is not the man Don Dionís is. Doesn't Portugal to this day weep for his father? You two will soon be one: May you be happy forever.

SERAFINA: Oh my Lord!

JUANA: Don't be afraid; my cousin has gone for Don Dionís. He'll be here soon.

SERAFINA: He has a remarkable friend.

JUANA: You can't find many like him.

(Enter Don Antonio in evening garb.)

ANTONIO: Now by love's nocturnal inventions I have become two men: a feigned Don Dionís and a real Don Antonio. I'll speak as each of them. Hold! I hear people at the window.

JUANA: There's a noise—my hopes were not in vain.

(Enter Tarso in evening garb.)

TARSO: My happy pal Don Dionís told me to prowl around to see who's about.

JUANA: Psst. Is that the Count?

ANTONIO: Yes, my lady.

JUANA: Have you come with Don Dionís?

TARSO: What is this? Don Dionís, eh, that's a good one! And is that Doña Madalena? He ordered me to look the place over to warn him if anyone was about. It looks like someone's walking around pretending to be him. Whoa! Maybe that's Don Dionís—no, it's not.

ANTONIO: Don Dionís has come with me. He's making ready the heart you've already won, so that he may offer himself up at your feet. Don Dionís, speak up, come now.

(As Don Dionís): Can't you see I'm stunned from contemplating such a glorious sight? To pay the debt owed you with mere words would be shameful, and so I've bridled my tongue, not even daring to use it. But, my lady, love is a god and he can pay my debt to you.

JUANA (aside): *He certainly can adopt another voice!*

SERAFINA: To pay this debt, don't you have some collateral?

ANTONIO: Well, I am not sure, but I'll give you someone who'll back my debt: The Count can go surety for me.

(As the Count): I'll be his guarantor.

TARSO: May the Devil take me! So help me God, he is only one man, but there seems to be two of him.

ANTONIO (as Don Dionís): I'm in great peril speaking to you here. Let my suffering come to an end and make certain all my joys.

SERAFINA: What do you want of me?

ANTONIO: I've already removed the latch from the garden gate.

JUANA: Be mindful that Don Duarte often strolls beneath your window. If you wait until day you must become his wife. Any delay is dangerous.

SERAFINA: Oh, my Lord!

JUANA: How shy you are. Shall I let him in?

SERAFINA: Do as you please.

ANTONIO (As himself): Don Dionís, love pairs you off with the greatest fortune it can offer. Be equal to the task.

(As Don Dionís): Count, my friend, through your cleverness and kindness I've gained the greatest of blessings. Let me embrace you.

(As himself): I am your friend.

(As Don Dionís): From this day on I am your slave.

(As himself): That is well.
(As Don Dionís): Time will be the witness of my debt to you.
(As himself): I'll await you here, so that I can come to your aid should you need it. Enter.
(As Don Dionís): Farewell, my friend. (Exit.)
SERAFINA: Has he entered?
JUANA: Yes.
SERAFINA: So this is the way love performs its will on a woman. But anything is better than belonging to Estremoz. May my father and my honor forgive me.
JUANA: Go. Banish your trepidations. (Exeunt Juana and Serafina.)
TARSO: What a tangle this is! This enchantment has tossed me into great confusion. One Don Dionís talking to himself said that he was staying outside and then went inside. He must be the devil.

(Enter Mireno in evening garb.)

MIRENO: No doubt he'll be sleeping.
TARSO: Someone has been substituted for you.
MIRENO: What are you talking about, fool? Speak to me: You came here to see if there were people about, and you behave like this, insolent rogue.
TARSO: People have been here.
MIRENO: Who?
TARSO: A count and someone with your name, some Don Dionís, who's one and seems to be two.
MIRENO: Have you lost your wits?
TARSO: By the Lord above, a man just went into the palace with your Doña Madalena. He's one of three things: a one-man language school, your soul in torment, or somebody somehow separated from himself. This fellow knows more than twenty Ulysses. Maybe some trickster has pulled a joke on you, or maybe I dreamt this whole confusion, or maybe there are two Don Dioníses here.
MIRENO: You dreamt it.
TARSO: Maybe you're right.

(Doña Madalena appears at the window.)

MADALENA: Has Don Dionís appeared?

TARSO: There, at the window, a figure.

MADALENA: Oh my God, I hear people. Psst. Is that you, Don Dionís?

MIRENO: I am that fortunate man, my lady.

MADALENA: Then come in, my shy one. (Exit.)

MIRENO: Now do you believe you dreamt all that?

TARSO: I don't know.

MIRENO: If my shyness was shame, then away with it. If, starting this very moment, I didn't get over it, then that would be stubbornness and folly. (Exit.)

TARSO: I'm beside myself, under some spell, and I'm leaving here in a fog. Two Don Dioníses have gone in or I've lost my mind. Puzzles like this one are forever coming out of these breeches; pity whoever wears these two baskets of enchantment. (Exit.)

[The courtyard of the palace.]

(Enter Lauro and Ruy as shepherds.)

LAURO: This is Avero, Ruy Lorenzo.

RUY: Here once I was rich and had many lands, and now, Lauro, I'm a poor shepherd.

LAURO: Time and fortune are full of ups and downs, both are inconstant and changeable. The Duke has a fine palace here.

RUY: He's just finished building it. A peculiar quality of old age is making things and not being able to enjoy them.

LAURO: Let's look for my Mireno.

RUY: It's still early in the palace; they rise very late here, and we got an early start.

LAURO: When did the eager heart ever sleep? It should come as no surprise that a father who loves his son rises early to see him.

(Enter Vasco and Melisa as shepherds.)

VASCO: For what purpose have you brought me from the rustic mountains to the palace?

MELISA: You'll know when we return there.

VASCO: This frightens me.

MELISA (aside): *Oh Tarso, you ungrateful thing. I'm drawn to you like tiny pieces of metal to a magnet.*
VASCO: How wonderful it'd be if some groom should catch sight of me. I'd swing by my neck.
MELISA: Oh, Vasco, go back.
VASCO: But why?
MELISA: Don't you see our master—if he runs into us, we'll never hear the end of it.

(The sound of drums is heard.)

VASCO: Let's go back, but what is this?
RUY: For what reason can there be drum beating so early?
LAURO: I don't know.
RUY: If I'm not mistaken, the Duke is emerging; there must be something stirring.
LAURO: If we stand back a bit we'll see what this is all about. It looks like they're about to make a proclamation.

(Enter the Duke, the Count, his people, a drummer, a crier.)

DUKE: Count, no news could give me so much happiness as this. Now the sorrows and travails of Don Pedro of Coimbra, if he still lives, will come to an end.
COUNT: Of course they have. May he at last have the fortune he deserves, a compensation for so many years of misfortune.
LAURO: What am I hearing, oh good heavens! Can it be me the Duke of Avero is speaking about? But no, I am too unfortunate.
DUKE: Don Duarte, before your meeting today with my son-in-law, I want you to hear the King's proclamation. Let us hear it.
CRIER: Our King Alfonso the Fifth commands the following:
"In all his royal lands let there be announced by solemn and public proclamations the punishment that took place in Lisbon of the traitor Vasco Fernández for his acts of treachery against the Duke Pedro of Coimbra, uncle to the King, a loyal and noble vassal who is to be respected as himself everywhere in the kingdom and his lands restored to him. Should he be dead, let his image be placed on a horse, palm branch in his hand, and brought to court. Any children he may have

The Timid Young Man at the Palace Gate

will be the inheritors of his patrimony. Vasco Fernández and his sons are declared traitors, and, following a custom dating back to the time of the Goths, let their lands to be sown with salt." (Exit.)

VASCO: That took quite a while to spit out.

MELISA: Yes, it took quite a set of pipes!

LAURO: Thanks, wise Judge, for your compassion, wisdom, and mercy in restoring justice to me.

RUY: With these tears pouring from my eyes I offer you my congratulations. Duke, may you live a thousand years.

DUKE: Who are those peasants making such a fuss over this?

COUNT: You folks, the Duke is calling you over.

LAURO: If my troubles sealed my lips, now is the time to unseal them. What holds me back? Illustrious Duke, my dear cousin, embrace me, I am Don Pedro.

DUKE: Lord, my thanks for this.

COUNT: A great duke in these clothes?

LAURO: Until now these rags have preserved my honor and my life.

MELISA: Whoa! They say our master is a duke.

VASCO: Yes.

MELISA: Let's give him our congratulations.

VASCO: Can't you see he's busy? There'll be time enough for that. Forget it for now, and spare us a scolding.

MELISA: Then let's drop it for now.

DUKE (to Lauro): To the Count of Estremoz I've promised my younger daughter in marriage. Now I await your nephew the Count of Vasconcelos.

LAURO: If my brother was deceived by traitors, no doubt he now regrets it.

DUKE: The Count will have Madalena for his wife.

LAURO: You've made wise choices in your selections of sons-in-law.

DUKE: And just as fortunate that you'll be witness for their marriages.

RUY (aside): *Even though he's seen me, the Count has not recognized me. How will my insults be avenged?*

DUKE: Call my daughters. They should know about something so strange that touches them.

MELISA: Vasco, it's true, come and let's go over there. (To Lauro): May you enjoy your "Dukecy" for many happy years.
LAURO: Melisa, here?
MELISA: I came to see Tarso.
RUY (aside): *I don't dare speak for fear of being recognized. My life is on my lips.*

(Enter Madalena, Serafina, and Doña Juana.)

MADALENA: What does Your Grace command?
DUKE: That you kiss the hands of the great Duke of Coimbra, your uncle.
MADALENA: How extraordinary!
LAURO: I weep for joy!
SERAFINA (aside): *I give praise for my good fortune. Now I'll enjoy Don Dionís without peril, for heaven has put an end to his misfortune.*
LAURO: Nieces, may you be happy forever with your husbands to be.
SERAFINA: May heaven protect Your Grace's life for just as long.
MADALENA: If you discover the slightest value in me and hope to see grandchildren kings to avenge your foes, I entreat one thing: Stop this marriage.
DUKE: What is this?
MADALENA: Though my female modesty would silence me, I must tell you this: I am already married.
DUKE: Good Lord. You impudent thing, have you lost your senses?
MADALENA: The conjunction of heaven and love has given me a husband, who, though poor and humble, is clever, young, and gallant.
DUKE: My girl, what do these words mean? Do you seek death at my hand?
MADALENA: You gave me a secretary and now he is my husband.
DUKE: Not another word! Oh the curses of old age! You vile thing! For so lowly a man you scorn the Count of Vasconcelos.
MADALENA: Love has already made him my equal in station, for love knows how to humble the high and exalt the humble.
DUKE: Death to you!
LAURO: Be calm. Her husband is my son and your nephew.
DUKE: What?

The Timid Young Man at the Palace Gate

LAURO: The secretary of my niece, your daughter, is Mireno, my son and heir, Don Dionís.

DUKE: My senses start to come back to me. This insult turns out to be a blessing.

MADALENA: Your son? What holds me back from kneeling at your feet?

SERAFINA: This cannot be. It's some trick. The man whose hand and oath he gave to me is Don Dionís, the Duke of Coimbra's son.

DUKE: Can a man be more miserable?

SERAFINA: Doña Juana can bear witness to my words.

MADALENA: Don Dionís is in the boudoir of my rooms at this very moment!

SERAFINA: What are you saying? Don Dionís is in my room.

LAURO: I have only one son.

DUKE: Bring these men here. In what a maze of confusion I find myself.

MELISA: Vasco, how will this turn out?

VASCO: I have no answer for you. I can't tell if I'm dreaming or if what I'm seeing is real.

MELISA (aside): *Oh, if Tarso should appear*!

(Enter Mireno.)

MIRENO: In utter perplexity, I humble myself before you.

LAURO: My son, throw your arms around your father and infuse new blood into an old man's heart. This is Don Dionís.

SERAFINA: Is heaven so cruel? What deception has all this been?

DUKE: Embrace me now that Portugal's gallant heir has been found on this land.

LAURO: Son, why so bemused? You've shed the coarse name of Mireno and I've Lauro. Now I am the Duke of Coimbra and the King knows that I am innocent.

MIRENO: What do these words mean? Heavens! Love! So many blessings!

(Enter Don Antonio.)

ANTONIO: I humble myself in your presence.

DUKE: Secretary, what accounts for your presence here?

SERAFINA: What's become of my husband, Don Dionís?

ANTONIO: You have been deceived by me. Last night, in his name, love's greatest joy you surrendered to me.

DUKE: Scoundrel!

SERAFINA: Slay him!

COUNT: Kill him!

JUANA: Be calm. He's the Count of Penela, my cousin.

ANTONIO: Duke, I kneel at your feet and ask forgiveness.

COUNT: All this must be the work of heaven, for it comes in defense of Leonela. I gave my word to her and my hand, possessed her, and then scorned her.

LAURO: This is her brother who, though with dubious means, sought to avenge the injury done her. Now he lives a humble shepherd. If my intercession is enough to soften the wrath of the Duke, consider it done.

RUY: I beg your forgiveness.

VASCO: And so do I.

DUKE: I command it.

COUNT: Receive me as a brother-in-law. The promise to Leonela will be fulfilled, as soon as I return to my estate. Where is she?

RUY: At last your noble spirit has emerged.

SERAFINA: And was that portrait of me?

DUKE: Count Don Antonio, give Serafina your hand. His tardiness has cost the Count of Vasconcelos this opportunity, and I am free of any responsibility to him. (to Mireno) You are some teacher of penmanship! But weren't you the shy one, the polite one, the quiet one? But which of these came to the palace gate?

(Enter Tarso.)

TARSO: Duke Mireno? What is this I hear? Don Dionís, I kiss your shoes. In honor of these happy tidings, these blessings of your wife and title, I ask you to remove these breeches from me. Put them on some statue of Judas on Holy Thursday.

MELISA: Traitor, ingrate, inconstant man. Will you pay me the love, suffering, and tears owed me? On bent knee, Duke, I beg you marry us.

TARSO: Is this man a priest?

MELISA: Order Tarso to love me.

MIRENO: So ordered—and with it three thousand ducats. And I make him my steward so that he may continue to serve me.

DUKE: Doña Juana is now my charge, and she will receive a husband. Let's go and receive the Count of Vasconcelos. For his disappointment in love, he will hear the story of *The Timid Young Man at the Palace Gate*. Whatever its failings, the wise man will forgive them.

THE END

www.ingramcontent.com/pod-product-compliance
Ingram Content Group UK Ltd.
Pitfield, Milton Keynes, MK11 3LW, UK
UKHW042015140426
5217IPUK00015B/1182